CONFUCIUS

CONFUCIUS

A BIOGRAPHY

JONATHAN CLEMENTS

First published by Sutton Publishing 2004

This edition published by Albert Bridge Books 2017

for
Fred Patten

ABOUT THE AUTHOR

Jonathan Clements is the author of books on Khubilai Khan and Chairman Mao, *The Art of War: A New Translation*, and *Modern China* in the All That Matters series. He has published on subjects as wide-ranging as the Silk Road and the martial arts, and his biographies of the First Emperor of China and Empress Wu have both been translated into Chinese. Since 2013, he has been a Visiting Professor at the Shaanxi Key Laboratory of E-Commerce and E-Government, Xi'an Jiaotong University, China. In 2016, he became the presenter of *Route Awakening*, National Geographic Asia's TV documentary series on the historical underpinnings of Chinese culture.

CONTENTS

About the Author...vii

Preface to the Second Edition (2017).............................. x

Introduction...xiii

1   Scholar.. 1

2   Teacher.. 14

3   Editor.. 29

4   Statesman... 44

5   Exile.. 60

6   Sage... 72

7   Idol.. 82

8   Phantom.. 99

9   Institution...114

Chronology.. 127

Confucius Says... The Last Word.................................. 133

References and Further Reading................................... 138

Notes.. 142

PREFACE TO THE
SECOND EDITION
(2017)

'Cherish your old knowledge, and strive for new, that you may be a teacher of others.' Analects II, 11

Two thousand years ago, the historian Sima Qian included a biography of Confucius in *The Grand Scribe's Records*, not in the chapters on eminent figures of the era, but in the section on royal houses. By doing so, he subtly elevated Confucius to the status once prophesied for him, as a 'throneless king'. He also set the basic details that have informed every other biography of Confucius written in the intervening two thousand years.

Despite this, hardly any of Confucius's biographical details are certain; even Sima Qian was writing over three centuries after the sage's death, and over a century after the First Emperor's purges that destroyed so many earlier books. The oldest extant source on Confucius, *The Analects*, was itself assembled long after his death, as were all other surviving books in which he is quoted. One was supposedly compiled from the personal memories of one of his followers, but if other sources are to be believed, its author was barely four years old at the time of Confucius's death.

I have walked the line between fact and supposition. I have outlined the bare bones of Confucius's life and trawled through the available sources in an attempt to place the disordered quotes in a chronological order. The historical Confucius is a shadow, sometimes used merely as a mouthpiece for later authorities, or a folkloric figure to be cherished, praised or ridiculed. Sometimes he is even more ephemeral, unmentioned by name, but believed to have been the editor or compiler of other texts. The most famous of these is *The Spring and Autumn Annals*, a history of his home-land that stops suddenly in the year 481 BC, when Confucius would have been 70 years old. A century later, the philosopher Mencius claimed that Confucius had personally overseen the writing of the *Annals*, and that his teaching was manifest not only in the subjects covered, but in the precise wording used.[1]

I have worked from facsimiles of the original ancient texts, as well as commentaries in modern Mandarin and English. There are several forms of 'Confucian' saying: the words of the Master himself, others' wisdom which he quoted himself, the words of others quoting him, and more apocryphal sayings that are merely attributed to him. In total, the classical 'sayings of Confucius' in works either credited to him, or which mention him, amount to some 227,000 Chinese characters – roughly twice the size of the New Testament.[2] *The Analects* contains 20 'books' of direct quotes and reported dialogues between Confucius and his followers. Two other books thought to contain the essence of Confucian teaching are *The Doctrine of the Mean*, compiled by his grandson Zisi, and *The Great Learning*, compiled by his pupil Zengzi.[3] This revised edition of *Confucius: A Biography* incorporates further details, including some of the impressive attacks on Confucius recorded in *The Spring and Autumn Annals of Master Yan*, once thought to be a forgery, but confirmed as a genuine after a copy was found in a grave in Yinqueshan in 1972.[4] I also refer to *The Essentials* and a few quotes from *Several Disciples*

Asked, two 'new' Confucian manuscripts that were found in an ancient grave in Mawangdui in 1973 and published in recent years.[5]

Beyond the books that bear his name, Confucius also turns up as a character in other works from his era and the centuries that followed, some of which may reproduce stories about him that were omitted from *The Analects*. This has led me to consult the tales that can be found in *The Annals of Lü Buwei*, *The Book of Master Mo*, the works of Zhuangzi, Xunzi and Han Feizi, and the *Kong Family Masters' Anthology*, a doubtful source believed to date from the early centuries of the Christian era.

For this second edition of *Confucius: A Biography*, published 13 years after the original, I have added three new chapters that continue the story of Confucius up to the present day. This takes the book out of the realm of biography (Chapters One to Six) into a discussion of the subject's shifting fortunes after his death. Chapter Seven narrates how Confucianism became a 'school of thought' rather than the musings of a single philosopher about the protocols of his era, how it developed into a state ideology by the Han dynasty (206 BC–220 AD), and how it came to dominate Chinese politics for centuries to come. In Chapter Eight, I consider the two most influential contemporary critiques of Confucius – the modernisers who regard him as an outmoded, conservative thinker, and the post-modernists who argue that nothing in his writings is demonstrably true. In Chapter Nine, I assess where that leaves us today, with 'New' Confucianism as a widespread influence in East Asian culture, and Confucius himself, or a facsimile of him, used as an unexpected ambassador for modern Chinese soft power.

INTRODUCTION

*'Those who set their hearts on doing good will be forever
free from evil.' Analects IV, 4*

Everybody knows of Confucius, but few know much about him.
Most Westerners are unlikely to know a single one of his sayings,
even though he is the most important philosopher in Chinese
history, whose legacy endures to this day. There are 6 million
people in the world who describe themselves as 'Confucianists',
while the broader Chinese belief system that Confucius helped
preserve has 350 million followers in 91 countries (5.5% of the
world's population, compared to the 5.25% who are Buddhist).
Confucius has also attracted followers outside the Chinese
sphere of influence, particularly in America, where his teachings
are seen as a pragmatic, benevolent system of ethics that does not
require religious faith.

Though he is often revered as semi-divine, Confucius himself had little time for thoughts of the paranormal. 'Confucius
did not say anything on the following subjects: extraordinary
phenomena, amazing feats of strength, disorder and the spirit
world.'[1] For him, there was no need for talk of retribution or
rewards in a nebulous afterlife. Instead, heaven or hell began in
the here and now, with those around us. Husbands had a duty to
their wives, the old to the young, and parents to their children.
If each remained benevolent, while the other remained obedient,

these simple rules extend out into the wider world, augmenting relationships between rulers and subjects, teacher and students, or ourselves and our friends. 'When away from home, treat all you meet as if they are dignitaries. Show respect to the common people, as if you were at a solemn ceremony. Treat others as you would like to be treated. Then, there will be no strife, either in the home or in the country at large.'[2]

However, this teaching is often interpreted as an incontrovertible rule, whereas it incorporates another important aspect of Confucianism – obligation. The emphasis here is on relationships, not hierarchies. For Confucius, tyranny of all kinds is 'worse than a man-eating tiger', and each half of any relationship is obliged to honour and respect the other. People were expected to know their place, but also to acknowledge that the higher had responsibilities of its own towards the lower.

Heaven has ordained a difference between right and wrong, and the true believer must always do what they truly believe to be right. 'Our lives,' said Confucius, 'depend on righteousness. If we lose it but remain alive, we avoid death only by luck.'[3] He lived during the long decline of the Zhou dynasty (1046–256 BC), the first, dynamic ruler of which had proclaimed that Heaven had revoked its mandate to rule from the last king of the previous regime. In proclaiming this 'Mandate of Heaven', the rulers of the Zhou had set themselves up as the very centre of a universal system of obligations and duties, not only of the people to their ruler and each other, but the ruler to his people. The Mandate of Heaven, in its way, was the tip of the iceberg, the ruler's visible authority and duties, which extended deep down through the rest of his society. 'Ruling by moral example,' said Confucius, 'will make you like the Pole Star, which remains firm in place while the other stars revolve around it.'[4] But such an idealised concept also contained within it the seeds of its own destruction – the sovereign only rules for as long as he adequately serves his subjects.

The Mandate is easily revoked in the face of bad deeds or unjust behaviour, and Confucius believed that previous bad rulers had been deposed through the withdrawal of Heaven's support.

Confucius saw no harm in acting out of kindness; he sought to make the world a better place by preaching righteousness at a personal level. In his ideal world, goodness between the members of the family would expand into kindness between neighbours, into truth within a community and ultimately a benevolent world. Such was the teaching and belief of Confucius. 'If you are courteous, your friends will not dare to be rude. If you do the right thing, others will have to follow your example. If you are always true, others will not dare to be false.'[5]

Few facts are solid. Even his birthday is widely disputed, and often we can only guess the date of certain events by incidental details. Despite these problems, I have done my best to strip away centuries of commentary to reveal something much simpler – the troubled life of a teacher who lived two and a half thousand years ago.

Chinese is a rich and many-layered language, reduced to meaningless monosyllabic grunts when written in the Latin letters of the Roman Empire. Over the centuries, one great tragedy of East-West understanding has lain in the fundamental difficulty of translating between these two very different language families. I have tried to shift any superfluous Chinese words into the notes, where they will not complicate the text any more than is necessary. I feel the pain of the non-specialist reader forced to make sense of a sentence like: 'Kong left Qi for Lu, where the Ji held sway,' and have done my best to simplify matters. On many occasions, I have mixed what translators call communicative and referential language – in other words, I have written what things *mean*, rather than what they say.

Classical Chinese is an incredibly terse language that summarises the spoken word rather than reproducing it. Like all translators, I have expanded the text for clarity. An original statement, such as '*self what not want no do at man*' (*Analects XV,* Chapter 23) cannot be left in its original compressed form, but needs to be unravelled into the vernacular, just as the Chinese would do themselves. The end result: 'Do not treat others as you would not like to be treated', should, I hope, make Confucius far more accessible.[6]

Similarly, rather than burden the reader with characters' birth-names, nicknames, given names, surnames, poetic names, honorifics and posthumous names, in three or four contradictory Romanisation systems, none of which will mean a thing to a non-specialist, I have simply chosen one and stuck with it. It is better, surely, that we know Confucius's first patron by his posthumous title, Duke Zhao, than it is to force a popular audience to memorise several appellations or changes in rank through his lifetime. Glosses for the original Chinese names and variant Romanisations can be found in the notes at the back of this book, where any readers who wish to be driven slowly mad may enjoy them at their leisure.

I have referred to the subject of this book as Confucius, even though the name was only created by European Jesuit scholars some two thousand years after his death – their attempt to Latinise *Kong Fuzi*, 'Master Kong.' In ancient China, what we now call Confucianism was known as *Rú* – 'Refinement' or simply 'Education'. Confucius did not see himself as the founder of a school of philosophy, but simply as the interpreter of the best practice for a scholar and a gentleman of his era. It was only in later centuries that his ideas were collated to form *Rújia* – the 'School of Refinement', as opposed to other philosophies such as the Legalists or the Mohists. Later still, *Rú* gained new suffixes, becoming an 'ology' as *Rúxue*, or an 'ism' as *Rújiao*. The term *Kongjiao*, 'Confucian belief', arose during the Han dynasty, but is shunned by some modern scholars, who dislike the implication that it is a 'religion'.[7] In his day, Confucius was merely regarded as the latest and most proficient in a long scholarly tradition that stretched back for centuries. But Confucius refined that tradition and codified its principles, creating a system for looking at the world that would eventually come to bear his name.

1
SCHOLAR

'At fifteen, I set my mind on learning.' Analects II, 3

Three thousand years ago, there was a war at the centre of the world. The powerful Shang people had ruled for centuries after overthrowing a former tyrant. Now, the ruling tribes of the Shang warred against the neighbouring land of the Zhou and were beaten back. After a while, the Zhou peoples realised that their victory was a sign of military superiority over the supposed rulers of the world and went on the offensive. The Zhou people overthrew the Shang and plundered the treasures of their royal city. They proclaimed that they were the new kings and that Heaven had willed it by allowing them to defeat their former oppressors.

The Learned King, and his son, the Martial King, were revered as great heroes, but their domain was too large to rule singlehanded. Instead, they parcelled out areas of land to their greatest warlords and most loyal servants, creating a series of dukedoms across much of what is now known as northern China. In the early Zhou dynasty the feudal lords obeyed their rulers and, supposedly, the world entered an enlightened age.[1] As time went by, the semi-independent lords gained their own resources and armies, eventually becoming more powerful than

1

their nominal rulers. Within three hundred years, the Zhou kings were a shadow of their former selves, huddled in a tiny royal domain. Their capital in Luoyang was regarded as a centre of cultural excellence, but the power of the kings was weak. The kings were 'Sons of Heaven' charged with ruling the world on behalf of the distant gods. For as long as they did not try to exert their authority too much, their former vassals continued to pay lip service to them.

The words we use to describe the life of Confucius, like 'king', 'book', and 'city', sometimes serve to mislead us with their familiarity. When Confucius was born, a book was a collection of bamboo strips held together with leather ties. Rome was still a collection of huts. Pythagoras had yet to develop his theory of geometry, Buddha was still not yet enlightened, and Jerusalem had yet to have its fabled Temple. Cambyses II ruled the Persian Empire, from where he coveted Pharoah Ahmose II's Egypt. The attempted Persian invasion of the West, that would unite the Greek city-states and lead to European civilisation as we know it, was still forty years away. The Zhou kings, who believed themselves to be the rulers of the whole world, were ignorant of these other civilisations. As far as they were concerned, there was the Middle Kingdom, where they ruled, and then there were barbarians on the edges waiting for the light of civilisation.

China in the sixth century BC was in the midst of a radical upheaval, based not merely on technology, but on the basic materials that formed that technology. The Zhou dynasty was a Bronze Age institution, but the Iron Age had begun, bringing with it a profound acceleration of social change. Iron allowed for the fashioning of more efficient tools, making it possible to clear larger areas of land for farming. The arrival of innovations like the ox-drawn plough, irrigation and fertilisers would see agricultural productivity take huge leaps, doubling during the late Zhou era.[2] The period saw a sudden increase in population and expansion of political interests, and iron would also transform the battlefield. Armies were growing in size, undermining the old courtly rules of engagement and unbalancing old alliances.[3]

Nor was China the monolithic state of later centuries, but a cluster of inter-related dukedoms. The nominal king dwelt in a small area near the Yellow River. Radiating out from the royal domain were principalities that paid homage to their symbolic leader, but were largely left to govern themselves. These in turn were often sub-divided into smaller baronies and city-states. Their ruling families indulged in unending squabbles over succession and territory.

Sources differ on how far the ancestry of Confucius can be traced into the past. It was certainly his own belief that he was a distant descendant of royalty. However, the blue blood in Confucius' veins came from the long-defeated line of the previous dynasty. The lost kingdom of Shang had been a small state encompassing the floodplain of the Yellow River.[4] When the Zhou had seized control, the last Shang king remained wilfully ignorant of the disaster faced by his country, but his elder half-brother[5], the son of a royal concubine, decided that it was time to cut his losses. Rather than stay for the inevitable end, the half-brother withdrew from the court, leaving his more belligerent relatives to resist their superior enemies.

He was eventually rewarded for his non-combatant stance. With the Zhou now ruling both their own territory and the conquered state of the Shang, the pacifist was co-opted into the new nobility. He was given the principality of Song over which to rule and charged with continuing the ancestral sacrifices to the departed members of the Shang royal family. By this means, the new rulers hoped to appease the vengeful spirits of the rulers they had overthrown. As Confucius' most famous and high-ranking forefather, this man was the subject of some family pride. Whereas a more military oriented family could have regarded such an ancestor's act as appeasement or collaboration, the relatives of Confucius regarded it as an act of honourable pragmatism. Nor would it be the first time that one of Confucius' ancestors found themselves turning away from violence and political intrigue.

Ancient Chinese peerage was fleeting. Few noble ranks were bestowed in perpetuity, but instead dropped a level with each following generation. A valorous warrior might win himself a dukedom, but his son would be a marquis, his grandson an earl, his great-grandson a viscount, and his great-great-grandson a mere baron. Unless someone in the family performed a new heroic service, they would fall off the list of the nobility after five generations. Such a system encouraged a more active involvement in government and warfare, but could also lead to acts of political desperation. Several generations after the last Shang noble became a peer in the service of the Zhou, his great-grandsons had their post stolen from them by their uncle. One of the two brothers accepted his fate and renounced his inheritance. The other entered into a feud with the uncle, eventually killed him and was invested as a duke.

It was another crucial moment in the history of Confucius' family, since he was descended from Fuhe, the elder brother who avoided conflict and not the younger one who fought back. From that point, noble rank began to pass through Fuhe's nephews and grand-nephews.

Fuhe's progeny were scholars and administrators, all of some renown, but without the high risks and swift rewards of their more aggressive cousins. By 710 BC, the ranks had run out, and Fuhe's descendant Jia reverted to the status of a commoner. We find him in Chinese sources still serving at the palace as the Master of the Horse, but with the mundane surname of Kong.

Despite a reputation for loyalty and uprightness, Jia met with a violent end. An evil minister coveted his beautiful wife and eventually had him killed. Jia's widow strangled herself with her girdle rather than submit to the murderer, and the tragedy led to a feud between the two families that lasted for several generations.

Tiring of the constant harassment, Jia's great-grandson headed north to the state of Lu, where he and his son both became civil administrators. So it was that, by the sixth century BC, the Kong family had a long reputation for scholarly researches, loyalty, modesty and a refusal to involve themselves in violence. Only one of the Kong family bucked the family trend, and that was Confucius' father, Shuliang He.

Shuliang He was a giant of a man, who had a long military career studded with accolades and dispatches about his strength and bravery. In 562 BC, he was serving as a soldier during a siege, and was one of a squad of attackers who charged through an apparently unguarded gate. The whole thing was a trap arranged by the town's defenders, who planned to drop the heavy portcullis behind the detachment of soldiers, and then massacre them within the walls once they had been cut off. However, Shuliang He was near the portcullis as it began creaking closed. Dropping his sword, he grabbed the heavy gate and kept it from reaching the ground, gradually lifting it inch by inch. Seeing the trap, his fellow soldiers were able to beat a fast retreat, while Shuliang He bravely held the portcullis aloft. Only when his comrades had made their escape did he drop the gate and flee.

The incident with the portcullis was probably the crowning glory of Shuliang's career. If the dates and stories match, he was already well into his fifties when it took place.[6] But as his retirement approached, the brave Shuliang fretted about his family line. His wife had given him nine daughters, but his only son, Mang-pi, was disabled. Whatever the nature of his disability (and Chinese sources limit themselves to calling him a 'cripple'), it left him in a state unable to carry out ancestral rites and sacrifices. If

Shuliang and his forebears were to be honoured in the afterlife, they would require a more able heir.[7]

After giving birth to at least ten surviving children, Shuliang's first wife was in no condition to supply another one. The couple had married young, but her reproductive life was already over. Shuliang's only option was to find a second wife to provide him with a son, and three candidates were available at the household of the nearby Yan family.

Even refracted through classical Chinese and over two millennia, Shuliang's meeting with the Yan daughters comes across as uneasy and tense.[8] The Yan girls' father reminded his daughters that, although the man before them was old, he had had a long and distinguished career. His immediate forebears were 'mere scholars', but Father Yan also talked up Shuliang's distant aristocratic ancestors in the Shang aristocracy. It would seem that none of this particularly impressed the Yan girls, who regarded the tall old man in stony silence.

Eventually, Father Yan reminded his daughters that he was keen on the alliance himself and asked them straight who was prepared to accept Shuliang's offer of marriage. The elder girls were wise enough to keep their mouths shut, but the youngest, Zheng-zai, retorted sulkily, 'Why do you ask us, father? It is for you to determine.'

That was good enough for Father Yan, and he promptly told the girl that she would do – her name can imply someone who is particularly outspoken and argumentative, there is a chance that this was not the first time the girl had answered back.

Shuliang's new wife was many years younger than him and does not appear to have been popular with her in-laws. One Chinese source even refers to their arrangement as a 'rude coupling' or 'wild union', leading later commentators to suggest that they were never truly married, though others have claimed the 'wild' part simply refers to the immense difference in ages.[9]

Details of what happened next are lost, buried amid century after century of writers' attempts to read portent and greatness into Confucius' birth. We only know that Zheng-zai, realising that her husband was not long for the world, prayed desperately for a male child. She also supposedly dreamt that she was visited by the spirits of the five planets, leading a mythical creature known as a *qilin*. Best translated in English as 'unicorn,' the appearance of a *qilin* was said to presage the birth or death of a truly momentous individual – a Great Sage. Zheng-zai's dream-figures told her that her son would be a 'throneless king', and the befuddled mother-to-be remembered tying an embroidered ribbon around the phantom unicorn's horn. Then she woke up.

Her prayers were answered when she gave birth to a baby boy, in a year generally agreed to be 551 BC. Confucius was first called Zhong-ni, ('Second Son'), although his mother nicknamed him Qiu, or 'Mound' after a little lump or indentation on the top of his head.[10]

Zheng-zai had successfully provided her husband with a male heir, but her troubles were just beginning. When her son was just three years old, Shuliang died and left her a widow. Shuliang was buried at a picturesque location, but neither Zheng-zai nor her infant son appear to have been invited to the funeral.[11]

By all accounts, Confucius grew up in genteel poverty, ostracised by Shuliang's first wife and family. However, his early life was not that of a pauper – Confucius did not lack for an education, and was acquainted with the local aristocracy, if not regarded as a member.

Confucius grew up obsessed with his reason for entering the world – performing the necessary rites to venerate his father and forebears. Despite the enmity of his relatives, the young Confucius made worship and ritual fundamental parts of his daily routine. Where other children played with toys, the young

Confucius reputedly played at religious ceremonies, laying out bowls and plates and claiming they were sacrificial vessels.

True to her wifely duty, his mother also saw to it that he learned the songs and hymns of the day, which served as an education of sorts, and possibly the only form of entertainment available during his impoverished upbringing. As an old man, he was once seen saying to children, 'Little ones, why do you not study the songs? For songs will give power to your imagination and heighten your perception, they will bring you friends and teach you irony. When at home, they will bring joy to your parents. When far away, they can bring solace to your prince. Moreover, they will teach you more of birds, beasts, plants and trees.'[12]

What family wealth there might have been must have gone on dowries for his nine sisters and the continued care of the disabled Mang-pi. The deprivation of Confucius' youth was just enough to give him a healthy obsession with frugality. It also left him with a recognition of the need for knowledge to have useful applications.

'What difference does it make,' he said, 'if a man can sing the three hundred greatest songs, but, when trusted with an official post, does not know how to do his job? If someone is sent away on business, but cannot take control, what difference does it make if he is educated? Learning must be of practical use.'[13]

Confucius appeared to inherit his mother's love of argument and his father's imposing physique, growing into a towering man, probably over two metres in height.[14] At nineteen years of age, Confucius married a woman from his ancestral state of Song. Although the couple carried out their conjugal duties, their relationship was stormy, and Confucius once complained that women, like servants, were impossible to please: 'Show them kindness and they take advantage; keep your distance and they sulk!'[15]

Nevertheless, the couple soon produced the first of their three children, and were congratulated by Lu's ruler, Duke Zhao (r.541–510 BC), who presented Confucius with two carp in honour of the occasion.[16] Confucius named the boy Carp after his lord's gift, and the poor child was known thereafter by the nickname Top Fish.[17] In years to come, Top Fish gained two sisters, one who died young and another who lived to adulthood.[18] However, Confucius never seemed to get along with his wife, and some sources report that the couple were divorced in their forties.

Confucius had attracted the attention of the nobility in other ways. Lu's aristocracy was composed of three branches of the same family, Shusun, Mengsun and Jisun clans, descended from the three younger children of an earlier ruler.[19] The Jisun clan roused his ire at an early age, when its steward, Yang Hu, snubbed him at a banquet by telling him that only gentlemen were permitted entry. He would make many comments about the extravagances of the family, whose ostentatious lifestyle was at odds with his frugal existence.[20] He was particularly incensed that the Jisun clan wasted so much wealth on entertainment, while seeming to display little knowledge of the correct protocol for sacrifice and ceremonials. For someone such as Confucius, who had been reared in the knowledge that the performance of certain rituals was his sole reason for existence, the attitude of the Jisun clan was liable to cause some frustration.

When he eventually found employment, it was as a civil servant, away from the back-biting and intrigues of the hostile clan. His first posting was as a humble manager in the government grain warehouses. With a wife and young child to support, Confucius threw himself into his work, and diligently kept records of incoming and outgoing stores. It was a boring combination of accountancy and management, with Confucius scratching records onto bamboo strips and checking to make sure that the grain stores were not under attack from mice or other vermin.

'My calculations must be right,' he said of his job. 'That is all I have to care about.'[21]

It was hardly a glamorous occupation, but someone in a position of authority saw that Confucius was wasted as a warehouse-keeper. Before long he was promoted to a similar supply position, but one involving the management of state herds and flocks.

'The oxen and sheep must be fat and strong,' he commented without relish. 'That is all I have to care about.'[22]

Confucius remained in government positions during his twenties, but his interest in ritual soon paid off in a new posting. In an age with pitifully little literature and even fewer people who could read it, learning was primarily transmitted through songs and poetry. Ritual and ceremonial existed to appease and persuade distant gods, but at a secular level, they were designed to educate – even supposed peripheral elements like statues, paintings, songs of praise, and the music itself, were all designed to inform the congregation about the world at large. In being an expert on religious ceremonies and ritual, Confucius was in effect a polymath. If there was anything worth knowing, there was a song about it, and if there was a song about it, Confucius probably knew it. His understanding of songs and poetry was at such an advanced level that he was able to criticise their content and collate variant versions to make a definite canon.

This eventually secured him a small coterie of students, interested in learning from him the correct way to perform the ceremonies. One of the first to join Confucius was a brash teen-ager called Zilu, who boasted to Confucius that his most trea-sured possession was his long, sharp sword.

Confucius replied: 'That, and an education would make you smart.'

Zilu retorted that he could cut down a strip of bamboo and sharpen it, turning it into a weapon that would penetrate the hide of a rhino – he demanded to know how education would improve this ability. Confucius pointed out that an intelligent man would have tipped the bamboo with metal and turned it into an arrow, implying that education would hone Zilu in a similar fashion. It was enough to make Zilu become a pupil of the master, though their relationship was often stormy and argumentative, particularly in later years when the nine-year age gap between them would become negligible and they transformed into a pair of equally grumpy old men.[23]

Zilu and others like him became the first recorded students of Confucius, although the young civil servant's sideline in teaching was put on temporary hold by the death of his mother around 527 BC, leading to a period of prescribed mourning. Since Confucius was only in his early twenties, his mother must have barely been in her forties when she died.[24]

'There are some things I cannot bear to see,' Confucius would say later. 'Narrow-minded men in positions of power, the performance of empty ritual, mourners who do not truly grieve.'[25]

The length of the mourning period was twenty-seven months, spreading across three calendar years, symbolic of the time that parents spent rearing a child until it was able to walk for itself. For the 'false mourners' Confucius derided, it would be glossed over as quickly as possible with a few perfunctory ceremonies and possibly some half-hearted fasting. Others, in search of an excuse for a prolonged mid-career vacation, would take the full mourning period, but use it as an excuse to avoid their duties. But the death of the mother who had raised him single-handedly was not regarded so glibly by Confucius. She had reared him as a master of ritual, and he performed the mourning ceremonies for her with the utmost adherence to detail.

He also took great pains to arrange not only for her funeral, but also to track down the site of his father's burial, exhume his father's and mother's coffins, and eventually lay the couple to rest side-by-side at a new gravesite. Although Confucius normally kept strictly to protocol, he broke with tradition by erecting an earth mound over the double grave. Heavy rainfall caused the mound to sag, and for Confucius to regret his sudden decision. If anything, it reminded him that traditions often had their origins in practicalities.

Confucius already had several disciples by the time of his mother's death, as he delegated some of the funeral arrangements to them. It was they who observed the collapse of his mother's grave mound and reported it to Confucius, who listened in stunned silence. Sobbing, the master eventually responded: 'They don't make graves like they used to.'[26]

Even though he had pupils of his own, Confucius continued his studies. With communications slow and sluggish between population centres, he took every available opportunity to learn from visitors from afar. In autumn 525 BC, the state received a royal visitor from a distant and puny kingdom, whose court was responsible for making sacrifices to one of the region's earliest rulers. Confucius listened intently as the dignitary expounded on the royal line of early China, and stayed long after the welcoming banquet was supposed to end, quizzing the visitor about the way in which his own country conducted rites and worship.[27]

He also conducted advanced studies in music with the chief bard of the court, since he regarded mastery of music as a metaphor for the growth of an individual. In the early stages, the would-be musician must be disciplined like a child. Only when he has mastered the basics is he freer to improvise.

'Music can be learned,' said Confucius. 'At first, discipline must be strict, all parts sounding together, but as the musicians develop, they gain more liberty to improvise. The tones remain pure and consistent, until the end, in several harmonies.'[28]

As he neared his thirties, he regarded his own skills as having risen above the basic. He knew the intimate details not only of his own state's protocol, but of the ceremonies of other states.

His quest for knowledge had started to pay off, as the attendance of Confucius at treaty negotiations or a diplomatic mission would ensure that his countrymen would do nothing to make the foreign negotiators feel ill at ease. Instead, he was able to present the actions of his countrymen in a permanently positive light. Visitors would see the people of Lu conducting perfect religious ceremonies. Songs and entertainments would not offend the sensibilities of guests from afar. Sacrifices were well chosen, as were the interpretations of the royal diviners. Confucius was able to ensure that official events ran smoothly and such a talent was extremely useful in an age when meetings were often held between armed warriors with battalions of soldiers ready to strike at a word. The tall, quiet civil servant's devotion to learning had turned him into a valuable member of the court.

2
TEACHER

'At thirty I stood on my own two feet.' Analects II, 3

Unknown to Confucius, his interest in education and his family's long-standing aversion to power struggles had reached the notice of the state's chief minister, Meng-xi. On his deathbed, Meng-xi told his successor that Confucius was wise indeed – whether he meant in general or in his avoidance of political intrigue is unclear. Whatever Meng-xi's motives, his advice did not go unheeded. After his death, his successor soon approached Confucius in search of further education, either out of genuine respect for his aptitude, or perhaps simply because the impoverished scholar did not seem to present much of a threat.[1] As he entered his thirties, Confucius finally found himself rewarded for his years of intense studies, not with a government post, but with a stipend as a professional scholar and teacher – two of Meng-xi's sons became his students. The ruling class of Lu were prepared to pay Confucius to teach them what he had learned and to fund further acquisition of knowledge with a research allowance. In return, Confucius appears to have served as an occasional adviser to the state's ruler, Duke Zhao.

Confucius was determined to put his grant-maintained status to good use, and soon put in a request to travel out of his home state to the distant capital, Luoyang. He asked for state assistance, and was given a chariot and two horses for his trip. By the standards of the day it was an immense distance – over two hundred miles, through at least two other feudal territories, whose alliances with Lu could not always be guaranteed. Confucius did not travel alone but in the company of several disciples, possibly with other members of the Lu court on diplomatic or trade missions.[2]

Luoyang was the religious centre of the Chinese world. Here, the ruling kings of China were responsible for the greatest and purest of rituals to the most high-ranking of spirits. Although the secular power of the kings had waned beyond repair, they still exerted religious authority. Confucius took great interest in the rituals of the capital, all the better to make the ceremonies of Lu as alike the royal centre as possible – his homeland was already famous for adhering closer than most others to the royal traditions, and Confucius seems to have been regarded as the ideal man to continue this policy.[3] He inspected the outdoor area where sacrifices were made to Heaven and Earth, measuring the grounds and observing the behaviour of royal officials. He also visited the Hall of Light where the kings would receive foreign visitors; there to check its *feng shui* – the nature of the building, its placement, and its interior design. In Confucius's day, a building's ruling direction, its entranceways and architecture were a vital component of political power in the human realm. From Confucius's later comments on religion, we can guess that he was less interested in the magic of kingship than in the way in which outside visitors were treated.

'There is more to ritual than gifts of jade and silk,' he said. 'There is more to music than mere bells and drums.'[4]

The halls of the kings projected their power and authority through architecture and decoration.[5] The walls of the Hall of Light were decorated with images of China's ancient kings reaching back into times of legend, each with accompanying notices on their vices and virtues. Nobody entering the hall could avoid gazing at several parables of past kingship, or indeed the most recent picture on the walls, which showed the previous ruler with the current king as an infant on his knee.

'Here you see how the Zhou dynasty became so great,' Confucius said. 'We study the past in order to understand the present.'[6]

Confucius also inspected the ancestral temple of the royal family, which he regarded as an equally important part of state architecture. He was not disappointed. Just as the portraits in the Hall of Light implied respect and remembrance, the ancestral temple carried that idea into the afterlife. Remembering the words and deeds of ancestors was of crucial value to Confucius, who lived in a time when so much knowledge was lost between generations, only to be discovered anew, passed on by word of mouth, and then lost once more. He was even more impressed by a statue in the temple that made a bold statement about respecting one's rulers. Crafted from bronze, it depicted a man whose mouth was held shut by three clasps. On his back was written a brief epigram about the virtues of silence.

'Observe it, my children,' he said to his followers. 'These words are true.'[7]

Confucius himself caused a stir at the capital, and dazzled some of the local ministers with his wit and decorum.

'When he speaks, he praises the ancient kings,' said an approving court musician. 'He moves along the path of humility and courtesy. He has heard of every subject, and retains with a strong memory. His knowledge of things seems inexhaustible. Have we not in him the rising of a sage?'[8]

For Confucius, the highlight of his visit was his meeting with the curator of the royal libraries, Li Er. The aged Li Er was perhaps the only person in China with a better grasp of ceremonies than the young Confucius, and the two men supposedly enjoyed a long meeting. Li Er, however, was not quite the mentor that Confucius was expecting. In fact, he was growing increasingly disenchanted with courtly life, and was already planning his resignation and retirement. Although we remember Confucius as an old man in his dotage, it is easy to forget that he was once young, too, and Li Er's words to him show signs of an older teacher reining in the youthful excesses of a pupil. Li Er thought there was little point in alluding to the successes of old when modern states refused to learn from their examples. He sternly warned the young Confucius that a political life was fraught with disappointments, and that success in his chosen career would only lead to enemies in high places.

'Those whom you talk about are dead,' he said, 'and their bones are mouldered to dust. Only their words remain. When the superior man gets his time, he mounts aloft; but when the time is against him, he moves as if his feet were entangled... Put away your proud air and many desires, your insinuating habit and wild will.'

Before long, Li Er's admonishments made themselves felt in a new twist to Confucius's own personal philosophy. He displayed little interest in the afterlife or the spirit world, instead concentrating on protocol in the here and now. Rituals served an educational purpose for Confucius, but he did not care for discussion of whether or not they could bring divine aid.

It is possible that Confucius's eternal sparring partner Zilu noticed this change in attitude, since he pointedly asked him about duties he had towards the spirit world.

'We cannot serve the dead,' Confucius replied, 'until we have served the living... First know what life is, before seeking to know death.'[9]

Over the course of his life, Confucius would allude on several occasions to things he had learned from Li Er. He also reportedly compared the librarian to a dragon, soaring high above mundane creatures, and immune to everyday distractions. He praised Li Er, not only for his wisdom, but for his policy of setting a good example for others.

'Good people must honour virtue and bring enlightenment to others,' Confucius said. 'Dragons and sages are not the only beings with the potential to know all and endure hardship. Be kind to those below you, let them observe your example like the markings of a Dragon – after seeing such a creature, few would forget the experience.'[10]

Li Er, however, did not remain in the capital long after Confucius's return to Lu. Instead, the librarian resigned his post and became a hermit. Referred to as *Lao Zi*, or the 'Old Master', he eventually disappeared, leaving only his writings in the *Dao De Jing*, the holy scripture of Daoism.

Confucius returned safely to Lu, and no doubt hoped to continue his state-funded acquisition of knowledge. However, the country was soon torn apart by a quarrel between its three most powerful families, and Confucius was no longer safe.

Nothing demonstrates the political instability of the time more keenly than the source of Confucius's undoing. According to the *Records of the Historian*, civil strife in the state of Lu escalated over a silly little incident. An argument got out of hand at a cockfight between birds owned by rival noblemen. In retribution for losing the match, one nobleman requisitioned the house of the winner, leading the aggrieved party, an earl, to reveal to Duke Zhao that the Jisun clan was lax in its ceremonial duties, retaining most of its officiators for the clan's own rituals, rather than rituals in honour of the ruler. The aging Duke ordered the arrest of the offender, only for the Jisun clan to bolster its position with troops on loan from its relatives.

Confucius would liken such flashpoints to birds making their nests in a house that threatened to catch fire. 'If there is a crack in the stove, the fire will spread among the rafters. Yet the swallows will not change their manner...because they are unaware that disaster is about to overtake them.'[11]

The quarrel masked other tensions. As Duke Zhao's reign drifted into its twilight years, nobles in rival families saw their chance to make a grab for power. Some demonstration that the Duke had lost his mandate to rule might be all that it took to get rid of him and his untested heir.

In turn, the Duke could not permit any insult to go unpunished. Although the fight may have begun over a sporting event, it soon grew into a contest over the state itself. When the offender resisted, the Duke's army marched in to apprehend him and discovered that many other nobles were prepared to back the rebel. In the skirmish that followed, the Duke's forces were defeated. After reigning for twenty-five years, Duke Zhao was forced to flee the territory he once ruled, running north to seek asylum in the neighbouring state of Qi.[12]

Almost overnight, Lu became unsafe for Confucius, whose association with the defeated Duke stretched back many years. With extreme reluctance, he followed his patron across the border to Qi, hoping that his sojourn there would be short.

Confucius had mixed feelings about the quality of life in Qi – his comments contain both words of high praise and embittered attacks. Such a bipolar attitude is best explained through the stress of his exile; with his homeland suddenly closed to him, he was forced to marshal contradictory attitudes. In the course of his short stay in Qi, he tried to make the best of his compulsory visit, only to face growing disappointment.

Nevertheless, a swift journey to Qi was Confucius's best option, and he set out with several of his disciples. There was safety in numbers, particularly with the belligerent Zilu as one of the party – a group of healthy young armed men was unlikely to attract trouble from all but the largest of bandit groups.

Confucius rode in a carriage, presumably accompanied by others of his group on foot or in chariots of their own.[13]

A wall separated Qi from Lu, but the borderland was lawless. As Confucius and his entourage passed Mount Tai, which marked the general border, they came upon a woman weeping by a grave. The group seem to have initially paid little attention, but her grief did not let up. Eventually Confucius called a halt to the journey, sending Zilu over to ask her what was wrong.

'You weep,' Zilu said to her, 'as if you have experienced sorrow upon sorrow.'

'It is so,' she replied. 'My father-in-law was killed here by a tiger, and my husband also; and now my son has met the same fate.'

It was certainly a sob-story of some weight, but Confucius, ever the practically minded, asked the woman if she had perhaps considered moving to somewhere less dangerous.

'There is no tyranny here,' she replied simply, much to Confucius's astonishment.

'My children,' said Confucius to his followers. 'Mark this well, oppressive government is fiercer than a tiger.'[14]

Borders in ancient China were often not clearly defined. In areas without a river or coastline to clearly mark territory, the lands of one ruler gradually melted into those of another. Confucius and his followers had encountered the weeping woman at the point where the authority of Lu petered out and eventually yielded to the sphere of influence of Qi. They had passed through the region of greatest danger and made it through unscathed.[15]

Supposedly, Confucius was soon able to tell that they had entered a civilised area. The carriage and outriders pressed on, past peasants working in fields and villagers dealing with their daily chores. Confucius was impressed even with the way they walked, commenting to his driver that the boy carrying a pitcher seemed to have internalised many of the teachings of the sages' music. No extant classical Chinese song records the virtues of correct posture, but presumably Confucius was either impressed with the boy's mode of lifting, or simply a gait that reflected regular dancing exercise. It is likely that something has been lost in translation here, and that reading between the lines of Confucian references to some 'dances', we should really be talking of callisthenics, exercise or even the practice of what would later be known as the martial arts.[16]

Confucius was ready to be impressed with the standard of learning in Qi. On arrival, he commented that he did not believe music could be so excellent.[17] By an accident of preservation, the court musicians of Qi possessed the purest versions of the original music of the Zhou dynasty. Confucius realised that the music played in Qi ceremonies was the closest possible match to the saintly originals of olden times, ungarbled by copying errors or later interpolations. He threw himself into studies and conferences with Qi scholars, and was welcomed by the local aristocracy.

Qi's ruler, Duke Jing (r.547–490 BC), had met Confucius several years earlier, when the Duke visited Lu on state business. The pair had discussed politics, carefully avoiding unwitting insults or slights by keeping to matters of ancient history. Confucius had praised the act of a legendary king, who once freed a slave and made him a powerful minister.[18] He meant to imply that the Duke should practise a meritocracy, promoting those who were competent in their jobs, and not alienating talented ministers through favouritism. The Duke was impressed with Confucius's words, which is more than can be said for his chief minister Yan Ying, who was also in attendance. Whether or not Confucius intended his words to be a veiled insult, Yan Ying saw it as such.

Years later, when Confucius arrived in Qi and hoped to presume on his earlier meeting with Duke Jing, Yan Ying had not forgotten their first encounter. Undoubtedly, he regarded Confucius as a threat, and seethed while the Duke welcomed his new guest[19] over the course of several discussions on statecraft and politics. Before long, the Duke offered Confucius a permanent post, suggesting that he might like to be given authority over a town. Confucius, however, found a way of declining the offer – although he had publicly praised the standard of learning in Qi, in private he seemed less positive.

'A gentleman only receives rewards for services rendered,' he confided to his followers. 'I have given advice to Duke Jing, but he has yet to follow it. And now he wants to confer this title upon me? He is very far from understanding me!'[20]

Conceivably, Confucius would have been more willing to stay in Qi if the Duke were prepared to listen to his advice, but none of his suggestions took hold. The Duke's initial agreement soon met with resistance further down the chain of command, as his ministers and officers invented obstacles and counter-arguments to discredit the newcomer. Paramount among the resentful opposition, of course, was chief minister Yan Ying. While Yan Ying struggled with the practicalities of running the state, and worried over the implications of the civil strife over the border in the state of Lu, his lord and master idled the days away discussing matters of mere theory with the new arrival.

Yan Ying and Confucius became open rivals – implicit in many of Confucius's dialogues with the Duke was his opinion that the Duke was being let down by his ministers. Ironically, Yan Ying may not have been the minister at fault. He and Confucius seem to have had more in common than otherwise. Indeed, there were incidents in Yan Ying's career that seemed to represent the pinnacle of Confucius's own ideas, most notably an occasion where Yan Ying and the music master of Qi refused to indulge the drunken demands of a foreign ambassador at a banquet. When confronted over his actions, Yan Ying said that the ambassador had demanded a tune reserved only for the King. Meanwhile, the ambassador would later claim that he had only been feigning drunkenness to test the mettle of the people of Qi, and that Yan Ying's resistance had led his masters to cancel a planned invasion.

Yan Ying 'did not move from amidst the cups and plates of food,' commented the admiring Confucius, 'but nevertheless he caused the enemy to withdraw their troops.'[21]

The Spring and Autumn of Master Yan, an ancient biography of Yan Ying, contains several similar incidents in which Confucius observes Yan Ying finding brutal, pragmatic solutions to impossible situations. One involved Duke Jing's unwise order for the construction of a new tower, despite terrible weather. Following orders, even though they were misguided, Yan Ying arrived at the scene with a whip to force the indentured labourers to get on with their work, only to be overruled by the Duke, who sent a command that permitted the workers to flee.[22]

Another incident was even more telling, with Duke Jing inconsolable at the death of his favourite concubine, refusing to leave her side. Faced with mounting political embarrassment, not to mention state events in suspension until the woman could be laid to rest with the correct rituals, Yan Ying lied to his master's face, telling him that he had hired a necromancer to bring the concubine back from the dead. The Duke was persuaded to leave the room and Yan Ying was able to bundle the corpse into a coffin and send it off for a funeral.

When the Duke discovered the deception, he was red-faced with anger, only for Yan Ying to boldly tell him that such a white lie was necessary to get the state back to work. Confucius commented that Yan Ying had behaved admirably in negotiating a way through the impasse: 'A gentleman's mistake is still better than a petty person's good deed.'[23] Even here, however, we might see how Confucius's judgement was sure to cause trouble – in praising Yan Ying's conduct, he had inadvertently dismissed the Duke's grief.

Both Confucius and Yan Ying were proud, well-educated men, and classical sources appear strangely contradictory about Confucius's time in Qi. Confucius praises the quality of Qi's ceremonies, but pours scorn on its ministers. He jockeys for a position as an adviser to Qi's ruler, although in private he complains that Duke Jing never listens and does not command the respect of his people. Most crucially, he embarks on a feud with the man in Qi's government who seems most like himself, butting heads and egos over matters of state, when cooperation between the two scholars might have solved many of Qi's problems. But even when separated by two and a half millennia from the incidents discussed, it is clear to the modern reader how Confucius and Yan Ying could so swiftly rub each other up the wrong way – Yan Ying was a serving minister with a difficult boss; Confucius was a theorist on the run who had never held a position of major responsibility, but was ever-ready with patronising praise or unwelcome criticism.

A surviving account from the *Kong Family Masters' Anthology* shows Confucius managing to talk back to his host *and* insult a superior minister in the space of a single conversation – hardly the diplomatic tact he was to show in later life. When a minister arrived late for a meeting, he offered as an excuse the fact that he had been obliged to defend an accused man from persecution by a local dignitary. Duke Jing was impressed, and boasted to Confucius that his officers were virtuous men – for even the prosecutor had been prepared to listen to a case for the defence.

Confucius, however, managed to marshal a reply that put everyone in their place. He pointed out that a truly virtuous official would have hired decent employees from the start, thereby ensuring that he did not waste any time on unnecessary legal proceedings.

'I spoke too soon,' said Duke Jing, suitably chastened. 'But had I not, how would I have heard the Master's teachings?'[24] Considering that Confucius had managed to belittle him, the late-arriving official, and the minister who prosecuted the case, it was a remarkably gracious response.

It was not the only time that Confucius risked over-stepping the mark in his dialogues with Duke Jing. The Duke, who was considering passing over his eldest son in the succession, once asked Confucius how a government should be best run. In his answer, Confucius took the opportunity to register his disapproval once more.

'There is government,' he said, 'when the prince is a prince, and the minister is a minister; when the father is a father and the son is a son.'[25] In the view of Confucius, the Duke was wrong to ignore the protocols of succession and his ministers were wrong to push their authority beyond that defined in their job titles.

Keeping things hypothetical, the Duke asked Confucius what would happen, say, in a state where such protocols were not rigidly observed. He wondered aloud if such a state would have the outward appearance of prosperity, but already be subject to rot within. Possibly, the Duke mused, officers would continue to collect taxes, and the government warehouses would still have an income of grain, but ultimately, corruption elsewhere would lead to waste.

'Even if I have my grain,' the Duke wondered, 'will I be able to eat it?' The Analects, where this story comes from, does not record Confucius's reply. Perhaps he realised that it was best to say nothing, and left the Duke to wonder for himself which ministers would be best replaced.

The Duke never considered firing Yan Ying, but was certainly pleased enough with Confucius's replies to try him out in a government position. Perhaps noting Confucius's former work experience in the state of Lu, the Duke suggested that the new arrival could be put to work managing one of Qi's feudal sub-districts.

However, this was Yan Ying's chance to fight back, and he did so with a long series of reasons why Confucius was not suitable for the task. Chief among his excuses was Confucius's relative lack of experience. It was all very well, Yan Ying argued, for Confucius to pontificate about ancient kings and ideal government, but platitudes about frugal living and just behaviour were of little use in the real world.

'That man,' said Yan Ying, 'is arrogant and convinced he is always in the right, so he cannot instruct inferiors... In spite of his great learning, he cannot use it to bring order to this world; in spite of his enormous concern [for others], he cannot use it to help the people.'[26]

Far from being a worthy candidate for promotion and service, Yan Ying saw Confucius as a disaster waiting to happen – an airy academic whose adherence to ceremonial and obsession with rituals would be a drain on more important funds.

People like Confucius, Yan Ying argued, were 'haughty and conceited in their own views, so that they will not be content in inferior positions. They set a high value on all funeral ceremonies, give way to their grief, and will waste their property on great burials, so that they would only be injurious to the common manners.'[27]

Yan Ying finished his character assassination with a reminder that Confucius dealt in abstract theory, while practice was another matter.

'Confucius lays such stress on appearance and costume, elaborate etiquette and codes of behaviour, that it would take generations to learn his rules,' he said. 'One lifetime would not be enough! To adopt his way of reforming the state would not be putting the common people first.'[28]

Yan Ying's hatchet job had a remarkable effect on his ruler. Not only did the Duke set aside his plans to offer Confucius a government post, but he also began to regard the visitor with icy detachment. The next time they were both at a public occasion, instead of chatting amicably with Confucius about ceremonial matters, the Duke simply ignored him.

The honeymoon period over, Confucius found other courtiers less friendly, too. At some point, it was made known to the Duke that, in terms of the strict courtly propriety about which Confucius so often made such a fuss, Confucius was being treated in a manner in excess of his actual station. He was a servant of a ruler in exile, and hence in a state of career limbo – neither truly possessing his original rank, nor actually bestowed with one of equivalent local worth. It was simply not becoming for the Duke to treat him as if he were a visiting dignitary. Instead, he was discreetly downgraded a rank or two, which in turn placed limits on his access to the Duke.

Before long, Duke Jing was heard saying that he was 'too old' to put Confucius's advice into practice.

'I cannot make use of his doctrines,' said Duke Jing eventually, bringing Confucius's unofficial probationary period to an abrupt end. The Duke, Confucius noted sourly in later years, 'had a thousand teams, each of four horses, but on the day of his death, the people did not praise him for a single virtue.'[29]

Confucius saw that he had no future in the state of Qi. Although the former ruler of Lu would remain there in exile till the end of his days, the Qi courtiers had made it abundantly clear that Confucius was not welcome. No longer appreciated at court, he could only expect an increasingly frosty reception as time wore on. It was time for him to leave, and with conflict brewing to the west, his only option was to head south again, back to the state of Lu, where his own strict rules of propriety would preclude him from accepting employment with the squabbling ruling families. Still in his mid-thirties, Confucius was effectively unemployed and unemployable. Nevertheless, he made preparations to return to Lu.

'There are three errors you must avoid in the presence of the honourable and high-ranking,' a much older and wiser Confucius would say. 'If you speak out of turn, you are behaving rashly. If you do not speak when you should, you are behaving deceitfully. But if you speak without first observing the mood of your superior, you are behaving blindly.'[30]

There is an apocryphal story in the *Kong Family Masters' Anthology* that claims Yan Ying had a change of heart. Confucius's long-standing rival came to see him while he was holding a banquet at his lodgings, and waited until all the other diners had left. When they were alone, he told Confucius that despite all he had said, the state of Qi needed men like him. He begged him not to leave the country, telling him that the state was in danger, its government like the driver of a runaway chariot, pelting headlong towards a deep precipice.

Confucius, however, had set his heart on leaving. He told Yan Ying that it was already too late, not necessarily for the state of Qi, but for the ruling clique of which Yan Ying was a part. Confucius was quite sure that the Duke would enjoy a successful reign and did not doubt for a moment that Yan Ying would live out his days in his post, but he expected their heirs would swiftly be supplanted by a rival clan. Throwing Yan Ying's chariot analogy back in his face, Confucius told him that he doubted that he could return the state to its true course, even if he was prepared to get out and push.[31]

With that, Confucius left the state of Qi behind – returning from physical exile, but with his political career in tatters.

3
EDITOR

'At forty I had no doubts.' Analects II, 3

Confucius was aghast at what he found back home in the state of Lu. With Duke Zhao absent, the three most powerful families happily divided up the territory between them. Since they could already do as they pleased, they made no attempt to make their usurpation official. They possessed a sufficient quantity of troops and officers to run the country to their satisfaction, and the feeble royal domain made no attempt to intercede on behalf of the exiled Duke.

Paramount among the victors was the hated Jisun clan, with which Confucius had crossed paths as a young man. Contemporary sources give little idea as to whether life under the clan and their cronies was better or worse than it had been under Duke Zhao, but presumably it was bearable for much of the population. There was certainly no revolt on the part of the peasant population; life for many in Lu went on as before, but Confucius was scandalised at the liberties taken by the de facto rulers.

As usual, Confucius regarded ritual as the cornerstone of all human activity. In his idea of the perfect world, the right king was in charge and ruled over a class of 'nobles' that truly warranted the name. Among the tasks of this upper class, in addition to management and logistics, there would of course be a number of important ceremonial functions, in order to ensure Heaven remained appeased and everything in nature remained in its proper place.

The situation in Lu could not be further from this ideal. The state's appointed ruler remained in exile, while the nobles who had defied him ruled as they saw fit. And the Jisun clan did not set much stock in mere rituals. They picked and chose from the available ceremonies, and could not care less whether they got things right by Confucius's strict rules.

Among Confucius's colleagues, there were those who criticised him for even considering a post in the corrupt administration. He replied with a metaphor to the effect that rescuing the drowning requires getting wet.

> The dragon eats and swims in clear water; the one-footed dragon eats in clean water but swims in muddy water; fish eat and swim in muddy water. Now, I have not ascended to the level of the dragon, but I have not descended to that of a fish. I am perhaps a one-footed dragon![1]

Despite this, *The Analects* reports Confucius sputtering with indignation at the behaviour of the Jisun clan. One ceremony involved a number of officiator-priests in a hall, whose job was to keep time during the service. Sometimes translated as 'dancers', these officers would clap, chant or perform a series of ritual steps, that both venerated the gods and also permitted the chief priest to carefully time his own ritualised movements. The number of dancers in a ceremony varied with the rank of the attendant noble – a great minister might expect four rows, for example. In the days of Duke Zhao, the correct protocol would require six rows, a number that would also suffice for anyone of princely rank. But under the Jisun clan, the Lu temple precinct had *eight* rows of dancers, an extravagant spectacle only truly worthy of a king.

'If he'll put up with this,' commented Confucius of the clan's ruler, 'he'll put up with anything!'[2]

Insult was added to injury by the choice of song at the ceremony. As Confucius listened in astonishment, the worshippers began a particular hymn that heralded the clearing away of the sacrificial vessels. The lyrics referred quite distinctly to the presence of princes as high priests, while 'the king himself sits gravely on the throne'. And yet, the true king was hundreds of miles away and there was not a prince in sight; such a travesty was an affront against Heaven. To a ritual specialist like Confucius it was an absolute disaster, inviting divine disapproval and who knows what else – fire, flood, famine, anything was possible while the Jisun clan were in charge.[3]

To some, Confucius's indignation may sound insufferably pedantic – in fact, he was regarded as such by a fair number of his contemporaries. But his obsession with ceremony was his way of pointing out a general malaise. As he saw it, if the Jisun clan was prepared to behave in such an ignorant manner towards religious ceremonies, what other liberties were they taking with their duties to Heaven?[4] Were the granaries being kept stocked in case of famine? Were the taxes being collected and the borders maintained? In an age of slow communication, the only clue Confucius had lay in the public behaviour of the land's rulers.

He also suspected, rightly, that extravagances like extra lines of temple dancers were eating into funds better stashed for more practical uses. One minister in the service of the clan reputedly squandered vast sums cossetting his pets.

'He kept a large tortoise in a little house,' Confucius pointed out, 'with little hills on top of the pillars, and representations of duckweed! Where is the wisdom in that?'[5]

Some disciples, sympathetic to the group that would soon represent their sole chance of local employment, tried to remind Confucius that not all the clan members were bad. Some, they argued, even behaved occasionally in a manner of which Confucius might approve, such as another state officer who famously thought each decision over three times before acting.

'Twice would have been enough,' grumbled Confucius, still convinced of the clan's fecklessness.[6]

Accordingly, Confucius desired no part of Lu's new government, although it is likely that Lu's government wanted nothing to do with him, either.

'Your time has passed if you are despised at forty,' Confucius said, and sought the company of those who did not hold him in contempt.[7]

Confucius went into retirement and busied himself with his growing coterie of students, and with an extensive survey of literature. He hoped for better things, and spent fifteen years as a teacher. Meanwhile, at the court itself, the usurpers reaped as they had sown, and soon found themselves barely able to control a civil service of unruly ministers. The ruler who would 'put up with anything' was eventually forced to put up with blackmail and imprisonment by one of his more powerful and corrupt ministers.

After such a meteoric rise to prominence during the ruler of Duke Zhao, Confucius's absence from the court did not go unnoticed. He was even asked why he did not involve himself in the running of the state.

He replied: 'I am a loyal son; I am a dutiful brother. These qualities are part of the running of the state. I am already part of the government, why should there be more?'[8] His words were an allusion to *The Book of History*, but they are often quoted as if they were his own, since they seem to contain so much of his essential attitude. He venerated his dead parents, he cared for his sisters and his disabled brother, and he tried to lead by example, hoping that if everyone did as he did, the troubles of the world would cease. One of the central tenets of Confucianism, lasting for two millennia since the time of the Master himself, has been that everyone has duties according with their rank and immediate responsibilities, and that if they are all carried out suitably, then the bigger issues resolve themselves.

'Never let your faith falter,' he said to his disciples. 'Love learning. If attacked, be ready to die for truth. Do not enter a place of danger, nor a state in revolt. When justice prevails under Heaven, then show yourself. When it does not, then hide your face. When government is good, be ashamed of poverty and deprivation. When government is bad, be ashamed of riches and honour.'[9]

The Analects gives us several glimpses of the lively debates that went on in Confucian classes. Posterity has given us Confucian sayings handed down as if they sprung fully formed from his brain, but many of his conclusions were tested, honed and refined over years of seminars and debates. Confucius encouraged deduction and argument in his academy – students were expected to defer to their teachers, but also to speak up when they had questions. All Confucius demanded of his charges was that they be willing to learn.

'There is no point in teaching those who do not wish to learn,' he said, 'nor in helping those who do not ask for it. If I present one corner of a subject, and my students cannot deduce the other three, I do not repeat my lesson.'[10]

Money was no object, either, and Confucius accepted students from all backgrounds, regardless of wealth or social status.

'If someone were to bring me a bundle of dried meat as payment, I would still not refuse to instruct them,' he said.[11] While his successors in later ages were often accused of snobbery and exclusionism, Confucius himself only operated on the basis of available facts. He accepted one pupil, Zichang, even though the youth had previously served time in jail. Rather than stigmatise Zichang for his past transgressions, Confucius welcomed him into the seminars and discussions, and eventually pronounced him one of his star pupils. He was sufficiently impressed with him to go one step further, and granted him his own daughter's hand in marriage.[12]

Later generations would paint an idyllic picture of the Confucian academy, with neatly dressed scholars wandering leafy precincts discussing matters of philosophy. However, the classes often took a more boisterous tone, and the *Analects* recounts several incidents when Confucius lost his patience with slow or unruly audiences. At all times, however, he still retained his caustic wit.

One pupil, Ran Qiu, dared to excuse himself with a crack about his own idleness.

'It is not that I do not like your teachings,' he said. 'Just that I do not have the energy to follow them.'

Confucius, however, was cutting in his reply.

'If it were down to energy, you could rest halfway,' he said. 'But you have not even taken the first step.'[13]

'No one heeds my teachings,' he once complained to his class in exasperation. 'I might as well get onto a raft and drift off to sea, accompanied by a disciple. Probably Zilu.'

On hearing this, Zilu was exceedingly happy – the older scholar was clearly smirking at the sidelines on that day.

'For Zilu,' continued Confucius, 'is the only one foolish enough to follow me.'[14]

The period is also the likely setting for the only sizeable incident reported in the life of Confucius's son Top Fish. Growing up around a father whose sole income stemmed from teaching, Top Fish became an unremarkable student at Confucius's impromptu academy. As his teens gave way to his twenties, the boy remained one of his father's followers, although presumably finances were tight enough that he had little other option.

As Confucius's followers grew in number, a divide began to appear between the generations. Long-term disciples such as Zilu often appeared to be closer in age to Confucius than to their fellow students, and the natural rules of propriety dictated that the younger disciples should bow to their elders in all matters. Some of the new arrivals, however, suspected that there might be a secret 'inner knowledge' reserved for Confucius's closest confidantes and hoped to find out for themselves what they were supposedly missing in class. Their searches, however, were to prove fruitless – hoarding knowledge for himself went against Confucius's personal ethics of education.

Nevertheless, the disciple Chen Kang approached Top Fish, the son of Confucius, and asked if his father had ever given him any secret teaching.

'No,' Top Fish replied, 'though once I passed my father in the courtyard, and he said: "Have you studied *The Book of Songs*?" When I said no, he said: "If you do not study the Songs, you will have nothing worth talking about." I immediately began studying *The Book of Songs*, but when I passed him again, he asked if I had studied *The Book of Rites*. When I said no, he said: "If you do not study the *Rites*, you will have no character." These are the only private instructions I have received from my father.'

Chen Kang was very pleased.

'I asked one question, but received three answers,' he boasted. 'I have heard of the importance of the *Songs*, of the *Rites*, and also that a true gentleman has no secrets, not even to share with his son.'[15]

Confucius had long been held in high esteem as a scholar, even by those who had little use for his researches or his advice. His long period of political inactivity allowed him to refine his knowledge to truly unprecedented levels. Fifteen years of private reading and public seminars gave him an unparalleled insight into the literature of his day. To modern eyes, such an accomplishment sounds little different from any other career in academia, but five hundred years before the birth of Christ, Confucius was one of the first individuals to ever live such a life. Formerly, noble families had appointed tutors for their children by finding specialists and paying them to give occasional lessons. In making study itself his life's work Confucius became the first true academic.[16]

In an age of few books, he also set about compiling approved editions from what material was available. His question to Top Fish about the study of the *Songs* referred to one of several extant books that he was said to have edited – a distillation of thousands of popular ballads into three hundred acknowledged classics. *The Analects* contains a couple of moments from what could have been the first editorial conferences in history, as Confucius argued about song lyrics.

'If I must take a single phrase to summarise the three hundred great songs,' Confucius said, 'then it is – *Let there be no evil in your thoughts*. If people are controlled by laws, and kept in line by punishments, they will merely try to avoid the punishment, but will have no sense of guilt. If people are led by good example, and guided by a sense of propriety, they will have a sense of right and wrong, but be encouraged to be good.'[17]

Confucius was particularly pleased with a song from *The Book of Songs* that had a ruler in ancient times gathering bark from the mulberry trees and fastening his dwelling before there were even signs of a storm in the sky. The terms used are so simple that it could easily be a village headman securing a lean-to, but for Confucius, it possessed the quintessence of leading by example. 'The writer of this song must have understood rulership,' he said. 'If he is able to rightly govern his kingdom, who would dare insult him? Today there is leisure and rest from external troubles, and the rulers take advantage of it, losing themselves in pleasure and indolence. They call forth disaster on themselves. Both good fortune and calamity are men's own seeking.'[18]

Confucius saw *The Book of Songs* as a broad and general education, and could never have known how its use in classrooms would ensure that its content would survive to present people of our time with a snapshot of the lives and loves of the Chinese of two thousand five hundred years in the past. Here is a sad and mournful ballad, the words of a widower to the spirit of his departed wife, as he puts a brave face on his loneliness.

How can they say I've got no robes when I have seven?
Clothes good enough for a man.
I'll be fine. I'm lucky.

How can they say I've got no robes when I have six?
Clothes good enough for a man.
I'll be fine. I'm warm.[19]

The old man boasts that he's doing well and that the concerns of others are misplaced. And yet, there are clearly already whispers that he is not properly taking care of himself. A wife, responsible for the manufacture and repair of her husband's wardrobe, is not around to look after him. Already his seven robes are reduced to six; already his expectations have diminished from the good life to merely keeping warm. Tantalisingly, the song breaks off with the implied countdown only just begun. We might imagine later verses with the count of clothes dropping from five, to four ... and so on until it fades into ominous, threadbare silence. Or perhaps the song is unfinished for a happier reason?

Confucius said: 'In serving your parents, remonstrate with them gently. If they will not listen, then increase your reverence, but do not abandon your purpose. Persevere, but do not rise to anger.'[20] What we first assume to be a song about death and decline might instead be a talking point on filial piety. There is no verse about a mere five robes, for the filial child has stepped in to care for the bereaved father.

A stickler as ever for correctness in all things, Confucius did his best to ensure that no substandard song survived in his approved repertoire. If the songs did not inform or encourage the best way to live in harmony with others, he dropped them from his collection. He is even reported to have rejected some on grounds of bad metaphors or illogical analogies.

Confucius rejected a song that went: *The flowers of the shadbush, Sway to and fro upon the branch, It's not that I do not miss my love, But her home is far, far away.* Confucius said: 'He does not miss her. What would a true lover care about distance?'[21] When educating the masses required a small but wide-ranging number of hymns and songs, there was no space in Confucius's compilation for bad grammar or muddy phrasing.

Confucius did not merely work on *The Book of Songs* during this period. He also supposedly edited the books *History, Rites* and *Music,* fixing centuries of tradition in the best of possible forms.[22] His students were expected to know of the great deeds of the kings of old, the ceremonies that kept the universe in balance and the songs and music that should be played at them, and by compiling all available materials, Confucius put his personal stamp of approval on much earlier tradition.

His reasoning was that the most crucial elements in human knowledge were the 'rites'. This included the ceremonies that the Jisun clan were merrily botching, but the word has a wider meaning in a Confucian sense; we might also translate it as courtesy, propriety, or protocols, and the correct usage of everything in its proper place. 'Employ the upright,' he said, 'and put aside the crooked – in this way, the crooked can be made to be upright.'[23]

The books of *History, Rites* and *Music* were important to Confucius for their use in education, to allow for a meticulous sorting of people, situations and responsibilities. This is sometimes known in Chinese short-hand as *zheng ming*, 'the rectification of names'. Confucius hated the empty rituals of his age; he wanted people to know what they were celebrating or symbolising, otherwise the ritual served no purpose. He was, in effect, writing the manual, in the hope that transgressors like the Jisun clan would get around to reading it. Understanding the 'rites', he argued, would ensure that everyone understood the workings and assumptions of their society. Understanding the 'rectification of names', calling things by their proper classification, would ensure that everybody knew their place and function within that society.[24]

The books that formed the core of his curriculum and were taught to many students, although only a few became full 'graduates' of the school, deemed proficient in all areas. While the Jisun clan continued to fly in the face of propriety, their rule oversaw the creation of a generation of scholars able to tell them exactly where they were going wrong.

However, the clan were not in a mood to listen. In 510 BC, Duke Zhao finally died in exile, an act which was, ironically, to prove far more damaging to the Jisun clan than attacking them with an army. With their nominal ruler now dead, they were obliged to mount ceremonies in his honour and also to appoint his son as their new leader. However briefly hopes may have raised, they were soon dashed, as the clans continued to ride roughshod over tradition. The Duke's son was passed over in the succession, and instead they selected Duke Zhao's brother as their new ruler. He was known to posterity as Duke Ding (r.509–495 BC), and his epitaph would eventually read: 'Greatly anxious, pacifier of the people'.[25]

By this point, several of Confucius's disciples were graduating from the academy and finding government jobs, both within the state of Lu and beyond. After years in the political wilderness, his absence from court life was clearly getting to him at last.

Earlier critics still stung him with their accusations that he knew only theory and nothing of practice. As he entered middle age, he had yet to prove that any of his ideas would actually improve the running of a state, although some of his disciples were finding fame by applying his teachings elsewhere.

Confucius still refused to serve the incumbent administration, citing the continued infringements of the Jisun clan as his reason. The two government officials whom Confucius most despised were Yang Hu[26] and Gongshan Furao, although the feeling does not appear to have been mutual. While Confucius busied himself with his scholars, these leading Lu officers made several attempts to offer Confucius a job. However, since they were the two men currently holding their own Duke Ding under a state of house arrest, Confucius was in a quandary. At one point, he even considered accepting their offer, on the understanding that he could do more good as part of a corrupt organisation than as someone who was not part of anything.

Gongshan Furao, who was then in open defiance of the ruling families of Lu, sent an invitation to Confucius. Implicit in the communication was the offer of political patronage – Gongshan had seized control of a town that belonged to the ruling families of Lu, and perhaps hoped to set himself up as the state's new ruler.

Confucius was an unenviable position, waiting for a noble employer, only to find the original usurpers now about to be themselves usurped. If Gongshan were successful, Confucius might have a chance of a post in the new order, but if he did so, he would be betraying his own rules of propriety. Instead of abstaining from action, he would actively defy the rulers of Lu.

Confucius began to seriously consider the offer, but was stopped by the arguments of Zilu. As one of the eldest disciples, it is likely that only Zilu was brave enough, or foolhardy enough, to stand up to him.

'But,' Confucius said, 'surely he has invited me to see him for a reason?' Confucius was aching to put his theories into practice, and tried to reason with Zilu, pointing out that if he was right, his influence ought to make any state eventually transform into something wonderful, perhaps even as glorious as the capital of the dynasty itself.

'If anyone makes me the offer,' he said, 'with my help they could become like the Eastern Zhou.'

At least Confucius actually considered the offer from Gongshan Furao before rejecting it. Other offers were treated with even greater disdain. One of his former pupils, an academy dropout named Ru Bei, came to see Confucius, pleased that he had somehow obtained a minor government post for himself. Confucius, however refused to even see him and sent one of his disciples to say that he was engaged on important matters, and unable to allow the caller to pay his respects. But as Ru Bei heard this information at the doorway, Confucius made a point of striking up a song on his lute and performing in a loud voice.[27] He made it very clear to the unwelcome caller that his current activity was anything but important, but certainly more a more pressing matter than chatting with a pupil who had rejected his teachings.

The ultimate boss of all these callers was Yang Hu, the minister who still held sway over Duke Ding. Although Yang Hu tried to hire Confucius, Confucius would not forgive him for his efforts at undermining Duke Zhao during his long period of exile. We might also observe that Yang Hu was the same snooty official who had turned Confucius away at the door of a banquet many years earlier, telling him he was not a gentleman, presenting the now-respected Confucius with an irresistible opportunity to make his life difficult.[28]

He was keen to bring Confucius into the government, and when Confucius made himself deliberately unavailable, Yang Hu was forced to resort to underhand means. He sent Confucius the gift of a pig, which arrived at Confucius's house when the philosopher was away. By Confucius's own strict rules of protocol, this now obliged him to pay a courtesy call on Yang Hu.

But Confucius knew the rules of propriety better than anyone else, and also knew ways around them. He realised that he could avoid getting into a political discussion with Yang Hu if he in turn managed to arrive at a time when the corrupt minister was out. Timing his journey carefully, Confucius set out for Yang Hu's house, practising his look of feigned dismay when Yang Hu turned out to be absent. However, by luck or by judgement, Yang Hu was travelling on the same road.

'Come, let me speak with you,' he said, although *The Analects* records no reply from Confucius.

'Is it right,' Yang Hu pressed, 'that a good man should hoard a precious jewel, clutching it to his breast while his native land falls into confusion?'[29]

'No,' was Confucius's terse and reluctant response.

'And is it wise,' Yang Hu continued, 'for a man to be anxious for public office, and yet constantly lose the opportunities of attaining it?'

'No,' came the reply.

'The days and months are passing away,' said Yang Hu. 'We are not getting any younger.'

'Fine,' Confucius is reported as saying. 'I will go into office.'

Although this is word-for-word how his return to government is reported in the *Analects*, Confucius still did not work for Yang Hu. But after fifteen long years of corruption, matters came to a head in 501 BC. One of Confucius's graduates would argue that it was inevitable – nobles were ignoble, ministers exceeded their authority, corruption was rife, and eventually the culprits would pay the price. By 501 BC, the three noble families of Lu had tired of their ministers' constant jockeying for power, and took back control of the country. Money, in the end, was the deciding factor – the families had larger treasuries to draw upon, and Yang Hu and his fellow corrupt ministers found their support eroding. Eventually, Yang Hu and Gongshan Furao were forced to flee for their lives across the border into Qi. Duke Ding regained control of his domain, and appointed a new, strong individual to replace the disgraced Yang Hu. The new chief minister was a pupil of Confucius, the boisterous, argumentative Zilu, and Zilu did not forget his former teacher.[30]

Before the end of the year, Confucius was offered a position in the government of Duke Ding, now restored to his true authority. After long years of teaching, and with his nemesis finally out of office, the philosopher finally had the chance to put his theories into practice, as chief magistrate of his own town.

4
STATESMAN

'At fifty, I accepted the fate decreed by Heaven.'
Analects II, 3

It was time for Confucius to put his theories to the ultimate test. He was given control of the town of Zhong-du and its immediate environs. Although the name implied a central location (*zhong* is 'the middle'), the town appears to have been in the outlying regions of Lu, somewhere near the border with Qi.[1]

The political thinker had been given a remote post, quite possibly in the liminal, lawless area where the authority of Lu petered out and the authority of Qi had yet to extend. It was a tough assignment, but it made political sense – at least he would be unable to do much damage if he proved to be inept. There were certainly those in Lu who expected him to fail – his promotion became the subject of a satirical song that started off by mocking his clothes.[2]

Confucius pushed his approved protocols on the local population, insisting on the performance of the correct songs at ceremonies, and the correct behaviour of people towards one another. He insisted upon due reverence for the ancestors, both within the family and within the race as a whole, and in his selection of songs and rites, he encouraged the dissemination of knowledge.

Science and technology have appropriated much within *The Book of Rites* that had a basis in fact; we no longer need a song to tell us the best time to sow crops or bring in our nets. The popular cultures of later times and dynasties have over-ridden much of *The Book of Songs*. Modern times have new heroes to imitate and new idols to set examples. The most obvious remnants of the ancient knowledge that Confucius prized so highly are now mere shadows of their former selves – Chinese astrology, fortune-telling from *The Book of Changes*, and the geomancy of *feng shui*. This latter discipline, for example, was once a subject of incredible importance, incorporating elements of geography, meteorology, and architecture. Beneath the arcane explanations and legends that informed it lay actual, practical knowledge used for siting buildings, predicting the weather and planning towns. Now, its most visible relics are simply superstitions.

When Confucius spoke of the 'kings' of old, he referred to truly primitive peoples. Whereas the English term summons up images steeped in medieval feudalism, Confucius's kings of yore are considerably further back in the timeline of human development:

> Formerly the ancient kings had no houses. In winter they lived in caves which they had excavated, and in summer in nests which they had framed. They knew not yet the transforming power of fire, but ate the fruits of plants and trees, and the flesh of birds and beasts, drinking their blood and swallowing [also] the hair and feathers. They knew not yet the use of flax and silk, but clothed themselves with feathers and skins.[3]

Confucius stressed throughout his career that perilously little separated mankind from such cave-dwelling forebears. The only thing that kept humanity from barbarism was a continued respect for knowledge, and, above all things, its preservation for later generations. Confucius instilled in his pupils, and in his new charges in Zhong-du, the debt they owed to the wisdom of their forebears. At some point in the past, someone had discovered fire, and because that knowledge was not allowed to die, some later inventor had used fire to fashion metal and pottery. Such developments led eventually to better tools, and they in turn led to the construction of houses, or the ability to cook food, allowing it to be preserved or seasoned. From textiles to armour, everything that Chinese civilisation prized issued in a line of innovation from the discovery of fire.[4] Confucius's teachings were an attempt to lock such knowledge in the heads of modern folk – language itself was the most prized of possessions, allowing current generations to build on the achievements of their forebears.

The rules in the *Book of Rites* took many forms, and at their most familiar simply repeat incidents of proverbial common sense. Boys were dissuaded from climbing trees or approaching the edges of cliffs. Parents should never tell lies in front of their children. Students should not interrupt their teachers while they are speaking. Good posture and deportment was encouraged. Travellers should make sure they know how laws differ in foreign lands. Customers at inns are admonished not to expect everything on the menu to be available, nor to get angry about it.[5]

The *Book of Rites* was also explicit on the nature of gentlemanly conduct. It dictated the accepted manner of dressing for dinner and correct forms of address to one's superiors. A ruling monarch was expected to pay his respects to local centenarians. In Confucius's time, it was considered presumptuous to address a lady by her personal name, and rude to present a knife to another blade-first. When a messenger arrived, there was a dress code for receiving him – a means of reminding the recipient that the messenger spoke with the authority of the sender.

Other rules sound stranger, and remind us that we are dealing with very different times. The *Book of Rites* stated that 'one
should not live under the same heaven with the enemy who has
slain his father', encouraging vendettas, but also a nascent sense
of justice – knowing that a victim's family would be obliged to
seek revenge, perhaps a would-be murderer might think twice.[6]
There are elaborate rules for the positioning of banners in chariots, to aid with identification of troop movements, and also
the correct rules of the road for charioteers driving esteemed
dignitaries.

The *Book of Rites* truly deals with every conceivable aspect
of life in sixth century China. One of its chapters even contains
detailed guidelines for dealing with fruit pips in polite company,
or how to slice a melon.[7] All of the above rules and regulations
were familiar to Confucius. Most of them were in existence
long before his birth although many transgressors, such as the
despised Jisun clan, merely cherry-picked the ones they liked. It
was Confucius who compiled and codified the *Book of Rites*, and
by all accounts, it was he who insisted on their enforcement in
the town of Zhong-du.

Much to the surprise of many, it seemed to work. Before long,
Zhong-du was flagship town for the region and other population
centres began to imitate Confucian policies. It was said that an
article dropped in the streets of Zhong-du would not be stolen,
but would instead be found by its owner exactly where he left it.
Men and women kept polite distances from each other. Funeral
customs were streamlined, and ostentatious burials became a
thing of the past. The Confucian experiment was a success, and
as such, it did not go unnoticed by Duke Ding.[8]

So at least, are the claims by Confucius's biographers, every
one of them a man with an interest in promoting his methods.
Many centuries later, it is impossible to say with any certainty
just how well his schemes performed on his test town – the only

evidence we have is circumstantial, since within two years he was fast-tracked for promotion.

Confucius was recalled to the Duke's court, where he given the title of Assistant Minister for Public Works, one of three branches of the Lu civil service – the others being Civil Affairs and Military Affairs. It was a relatively minor post, but it kept him at the centre of government, where he was able to speak directly with Duke Ding.

The Analects preserves one of their debates, in which the Duke asked Confucius whether there was a single slogan that could make a nation flourish.

'It takes more than one sentence to have such an effect,' Confucius replied. 'However, it is often said that "being a ruler is hard, and ministers face many difficulties". If a ruler takes this phrase to heart, and does not expect his job to be easy, prosperity may ensue.'

The Duke then asked if there were a slogan that could bring a country down. Confucius replied: 'It takes more than one sentence to have such an effect, unless it the ruler says to himself: "The only good thing about being in charge is that nobody opposes me." If the ruler is wise and nobody opposes him, then it makes no difference. But if he makes mistakes and nobody opposes him, this attitude will eventually destroy his country.'[9]

Confucius, however, did not give up teaching during this period. He gained a new teenage protégé in the form of his disciple and assistant Yan Hui,[10] a cousin on his mother's side. Yan Hui was the diametrical opposite of the argumentative Zilu. Where the brash Zilu was a former soldier who thought of Confucius as a peer, the shy young Yan Hui only knew him as the revered teacher and minister.

'Yan Hui is no help to me,' Confucius once joked, 'because he always agrees with everything I say.'[11] Nevertheless, Confucius doted on the boy, since he saw that the quiet, reserved youth internalised everything he learned.

'I can talk with Yan Hui all day, and he will nod at everything I say, as if he were an idiot,' Confucius said. 'But when he goes home, I watch the way he behaves away from me, and I see that he puts my teachings to their proper use. That Hui is not foolish at all.'[12]

In the shy, retiring Yan Hui, Confucius saw a diplomatic wisdom very different from the bumptious face he himself had presented to the world as a younger man. He saw that silence often had its advantages.

'When my presence is required,' he said to Yan Hui, 'I come forth. When it is not, I do not show my face. You and I are unique in that regard.'[13]

However, the old Confucius still made his presence felt. When the body of Duke Zhao was returned to Lu for burial, it was interred in the cemetery of the Duke's ancestors. However, certain members of the Jisun clan, unable to lay aside the enmity that had consumed them all their lives, ordered that the Duke's tomb be placed at a distance from the others. It was an insult literally beyond the grave, using the rules of *feng shui* to shun Duke Zhao, so that even in death he might not find peace.[14]

Confucius was in a quandary. As a minister for Public Works, the burial was one of his duties, but as a former servant of Duke Zhao, he could not bear to cause his late lord any undue suffering in the afterlife. Eventually, he found a compromise solution, and did as he was ordered. But once the grave was dug and Duke Zhao laid to rest, Confucius ordered the digging of a ditch to surround the entire cemetery. By delineating a boundary that incorporated both the original ancestral tombs and the isolated duke, the ditch made them one unified whole again.

The leader of the Jisun clan demanded an explanation, and Confucius told him that it was his way of atoning for his own disloyalty to his former master. It was a tense moment, but Confucius somehow got away with it. He had successfully manipulated protocol to save his face and his own skin, and such a stand seems to have even impressed those who disliked him.

In 500 BC, Confucius was called to attend the most important meeting of his career, guaranteed to test every element of his knowledge. Duke Ding was heading to the village of Jiagu for an important summit with the ruler of another state.

After over a century of antagonism, guarded détente and renewed belligerence, the state of Qi announced it was finally prepared to enter into a lasting treaty with Lu. This was good news for Duke Ding, as he would finally be able to secure guarantees from his opposite number, Duke Jing. Qi accounted for over half of Lu's borders, so an agreement between the two nations would free up considerable manpower and resources for defence elsewhere. Confucius, however, was suspicious.

Qi, after all, had been a place of refuge for every disenchanted member of Lu's government for generations. Nobody could deny that – Confucius himself had spent some time there when he accompanied Duke Zhao in exile. Now Lu's new ruler hoped to deal with a nation that had offered asylum to some of his worst enemies, including the traitorous former ministers Yang Hu and Gongshan Furao.

It was understood that both Dukes could bring their favoured ministers as assistants for the summit, to ensure that correct protocols were followed. Confucius was the obvious choice to accompany Duke Ding, and he was selected as the Master of Ceremonies. However, his presence in the Lu delegation was not welcomed by the men of Qi, many of whom remembered him from his earlier sojourn in their country. Confucius's suspicions were well-founded, since the men of Qi had every intention of hijacking the summit.

Chinese history in the time of Confucius and the centuries immediately following has a lot of odd moments like this – banquets or ceremonies that threaten turn into battles. It is often difficult to visualise, particularly in our modern age of remote warfare, the sheer tension and pageantry that might have accompanied a diplomatic 'meeting' in the Zhou dynasty. Two opposing forces with something to discuss would meet on neutral ground, often bringing with them entourages of charioteers and archers, soldiers and heavies. Their interactions might be entirely benign, although who is to say that one's words are not more persuasive when backed by shining cohorts of well-drilled warriors, their flags fluttering menacingly in the breeze? The two sides might make a show of their shared culture by enacting a ritual in the name of the distant ruler of the Zhou, at which point a mastery of protocols and practice would become something of an intellectual weapon. Who stood where? Who stood first? Who was the best servant of the King, and most deserving of the moral high ground in whatever discussions then followed? And if things turned sour, it was not a merely matter of a slammed door or a harsh word – there was an *army* waiting outside.[15]

We should bear such issues in the case of the Jiagu conference, for which the various parties had agreed, at least in principle, to show up without military backing. Plotting to kidnap Duke Ding, the state of Qi planned to arrange a distraction through third parties, namely the barbarian inhabitants of the region, which was of course excusably lawless. The Qi delegation convinced a group of local barbarians to head for the meeting place and seize Duke Ding.

Confucius, however, saw the approaching soldiers, and immediately raised the subject.

'Our two princes have come in peace,' he said accusingly to the rival delegation. 'If you have brought savages to disturb this conference, it is no way for Qi to bring law and order to the kingdom. Such men have no place in a meeting between cultured representatives. They are your underlings, and not empowered to participate. Moreover, weapons are forbidden at a summit – their presence is an affront to the gods, and contrary to common decency. In human terms, it is also rather rude.'[16]

Confucius's appeal to the laws of protocol forced a reply from the ruler of Qi. Duke Jing could no longer sit there and feign ignorance of the purpose of the approaching men. True enough, they were barbarians, but they were also his subjects, and they were advancing on the meeting place while bearing arms. The laws of protocol demanded that he order them away, and he did so.

Negotiations proceeded on the treaty, and Confucius was able to gain further ground with the rattled ambassadors of Qi. In return for amity, Qi demanded that Duke Ding agree to send three hundred chariots in support of any campaigns Qi might take against a common enemy. On behalf of his lord, Confucius agreed, but appended a rider. In return, Qi was forced to secede a contested territory north of the Wei river, which passed back into the hands of Lu.

It was an unprecedented diplomatic coup. The promised three hundred chariots were only an abstract concept that did not require immediate delivery, whereas the real estate was palpable – Confucius had conquered part of Qi without a single casualty.

Qi's ruler, Duke Jing, hoping to seize the advantage when his rivals were otherwise occupied, suggested that the two new 'allies' should seal their agreement with a lavish celebration. Confucius gracefully declined, reminding the men of Qi that, according to the strict rules of protocol, such an entertainment would be unseemly after so solemn a contract. He then hurried his lord out of the dangerous situation before anyone could protest.

Finally, Confucius could demonstrate the power of learning in action and he was soon rewarded with further promotion, to a post analogous to prime minister. Technically, it was head of the Ministry of Justice, but since the Ministries of Public Works, Military Affairs and Civil Affairs were each commanded by a hereditary appointee from each of the three main clans, it was the highest rank available to a commoner in the state.[17]

Across the border in Qi, Duke Jing, who had once almost hired him, greeted the news of his appointment with some concern. He asked his aging counsellor Yan Ying, Confucius's most bitter rival, whether the promotion of such a learned man to such a powerful position would spell trouble. Yan Ying replied with one last devious scheme.

> You have nothing to worry about, my lord. The ruler of Lu is a weak master; Confucius is a sagacious Prime Minister. You had better secretly show your great respect for Confucius and [pretend that] you will appoint him as Prime Minister of Qi. When Confucius finds that his strong remonstrance [to the ruler of Lu] goes unheard, he will certainly behave arrogantly... You can then refuse to take him in. He will have burnt his boats with respect to Lu, but without having found a new master... Confucius will find himself in serious trouble.[18]

The thorniest legal case presented to Confucius during his tenure was one in which a father sued his own son. It tested the very foundations of Confucius's teachings, since the Master had drilled his disciples for years on the primary importance of filial piety. Children were obliged to serve their parents with utmost devotion – the strict rules of propriety for mourning were merely an outward manifestation of the type of respect for elders that Confucius's teachings demanded. For Confucius, the family home was a microcosm of the state itself, and if children were obeying their parents, and parents were obeying their government, and the government was in the hands of just and honourable men serving an enlightened ruler, then there could be no discord under heaven.

However, the case of the father's suit brought Confucius's rhetoric to a staggering halt. He consulted with his advisers, argued it out with a few former pupils, and then left both father and son in jail for three months. At the end of their incarceration, he planned to simply release them both. Seeing this for the compromise it was, Duke Ding asked for an explanation.

'You once said that in a state or in a family, filial duty was the first thing to be insisted on. What hinders you now from putting to death this unfilial son as an example to all the people?'

Confucius's reply cut to the heart of his philosophy.

'There is no justice,' he replied, 'if we execute underlings for the failings of their superiors. This father has not taught his son to be filial – listening to his charge would require the punishment of the blameless. The manners of this age have long been in a sad condition; we cannot expect the people not to be transgressing the laws.'[19]

For Confucius, 'duty' was a two-way street. Sons were obliged to be loyal to their fathers, and commoners to their lords, but the authority figures had duties of their own. Privilege brought its own responsibilities.

'To keep order in the world,' wrote an ancient Confucian scholar, 'you must keep order within your family. You cannot teach others if you cannot even teach your own flesh and blood. Without even leaving your home, you can improve the world. Where filial piety is encouraged, the rulers shall be honoured. Where younger children acknowledge their duty to the elder, there shall be harmony in the world at large. Where there is kindness within the home, it shall spread through the mass of the people.'[20]

In the generations that came after Confucius, many forgot this most central of his teachings. Just as the tyrants of old were overthrown because they abused their power, Confucianism cautioned its adherents to do right by those less fortunate than themselves.

The case also illustrates one of Confucianism's fundamental flaws. Like any theoretical system, it is prone to human error. It posits the way that things were supposed to work in a harmonious utopia, but was imposed upon a world of mere mortals.

When pressed on this in later life, Confucius even provided a timescale.

'If someone were to employ me,' he said, 'we would see positive effects after twelve months. Within three years, we would have perfect government.'[21] But even Confucius recognised that perfect government would not result in overnight success.

'It is said that with good people in charge, one after the other, for a hundred years, there would be no need for capital punishment,' he conceded, 'for thieves and murderers would be a thing of the past. But even if a truly virtuous leader arises, it would still take time – perhaps a whole generation for virtue to prevail.'[22]

In other words, Confucius was fighting a losing battle. He had achieved much in office, but did not stay in his post for the minimum three years required. His use of the word 'employ' also carried with it a sense of obligation in both directions – he would carry out his responsibilities, but he expected his noble masters to approve his decisions. While the three Clans enjoyed watching Confucian reforms reap positive benefits in their country, they were less keen to allow changes that would affect them directly.

Confucius, however, pushed for full reform. He argued that one of the greatest problems in the state of Lu stemmed from the antagonistic relationship between the three leading clans. In much the same way as the Dukes could ignore the decrees of the distant King when it suited them, the ruler of Lu often found his fellow nobles defying him. The 'Mandate of Heaven', such as it was in Lu, only allowed the nobles to command the commoners. The Duke himself was unable to command the lesser nobles with any efficacy, because at the first sign of an unwelcome decree, his relatives would threaten revolt. This, in turn, was made easier because of the martial footing in Lu – each of the clans possessed heavily fortified towns allowing them to mount an armed resistance.

Confucius wanted to pull down the fortifications of the clan cities, so that only the Duke possessed a defensible site. Such a measure, while initially unwelcome, would strengthen the Duke's hold over his vassals and prevent them from opposing any further reforms. It would also prevent upstarts like the lately departed Yang Hu from seizing towns and using them to foment revolt.

The noble families, of course, hated the idea, but Duke Ding saw its merits. His advisers agreed it would be an excellent idea – unsurprisingly, since by this time both Zilu and Ran Qiu, the one-time idle student, had become government officials.

Thanks to the support of his clique and the Duke, Confucius was able to institute the first phase of his scheme. The Shusun clan complied almost immediately, but Confucius ran into trouble with the Jisun clan, whose city was in the hands of a former ally of Yang Hu. The Jisun clan put up a fight, sending out an army against Duke Ding's capital.[23]

It must have been a terrifying moment for Confucius, seeing the concrete, palpable result of his protocols – an army advancing towards him. It was a brutal reminder to the philosopher that until such time as he had his century of perfect government, political issues would still be decided and backed by armed men.

Duke Ding was forced to hide with his ministers in a tower, while his soldiers fought with the attacking Jisun clan. Eventually, the ruler's forces were successful, and the walls of the town were pulled down.

That only left the Mengsun clan, the ruler of which proved just as reluctant. Ironically demonstrating exactly why Confucius disapproved of fortified vassal towns, the leader of the Mengsun clan changed his mind and sat in resolute defiance behind his walls. Duke Ding sent soldiers to besiege the town, in a stand-off that wore on and on, eventually undermining Confucius's good standing at the court.[24]

The Mengsun clan would eventually retain its walls, but by that time, Confucius was not around to protest. Two years into his role as prime minister, he was forced to face another enemy he could not defeat.[25]

Over the border in the state of Qi, its ruler Duke Jing was still smarting from the embarrassing conference. He was also considerably worried about the demilitarisation reforms Confucius was busily instituting. However unpleasant their implementation, if successful they would ultimately fuse Lu into one single cohesive state, instead of the patchwork of rival families it had always been. Without separate towns to defend, the people of Lu would be forced to unite in a single common goal – the defence of their entire realm. The only wall worth holding would be the 'Qi wall' that ran along the border separating the two states. Qi would no longer be able to play clan against clan any more, and would be forced to withdraw from areas of disputed territory.[26] This, as the court of Qi all agreed, was all the fault of that upstart Confucius. More worryingly for them, if the three clans were forced to present a united front, the military might of Lu could effectively triple in size. While Confucius's well-intentioned followers were in charge, this would not be a problem, but what if a more martial Duke took over the state?

Duke Jing was ready to shrink his borders back to a more defensible position when he was stopped by his adviser, Li Zi. As a last-ditch measure, Li Zi suggested killing with kindness. If his plot failed, then Duke Jing could consider offers of territory.[27]

As a token of mutual admiration, Duke Jing sent Lu sixty dappled ponies, and eighty dancing girls. It was the women who were the secret weapon, hand-picked for their astounding beauty and dressed in the finest clothes available. True to the rules of propriety, Lu's Duke Ding made no attempt to receive them, but the leader of the Jisun clan sneaked out of town to see for himself. He reported the women's desirability to Duke Ding, who was unable to resist.[28]

'Master, it is time to leave,' said Zilu, his military upbringing him apparently leaving him with an intuitive sense of danger.[29]

Confucius, however, was prepared to give his master the benefit of the doubt.

'The Duke will soon be sacrificing to heaven and earth,' he said. 'If he presents portions of the offerings to the ministers, I can stay.'

Confucius's faith in his master's piety was unfounded. In fact, there weren't any sacrifices for three days. Instead of performing his sacred duties in the rituals that maintained harmony between heaven and earth, Duke Ding and his cronies busied themselves with their new playthings.

Confucius was deeply distrustful of the new arrivals, rightly believing them to be agents of Qi deliberately sent to drive him and Duke Ding apart. His last act in his brief political career was a public resignation, designed to shame the nobles into paying attention.

The nobles did not ignore Confucius's departure, but had other things on their minds. Half-heartedly, the leader of the Jisun clan sent a messenger after the departing Confucius, inquiring after his sudden departure. It was what Confucius had hoped for – he had made it easy for the messenger to catch up with him by staying overnight in a nearby town instead of hastening on the road. His reply, carefully calculated not to point fingers or name names, came in the form of one of the many old verses he had learned in his compilation of the *Book of Songs*:

> A woman's tongue
> Can cost a man his post
> A woman's words
> Can cost a man his head.[30]

Confucius was in no mood to hang around while courtesans from an old enemy enticed Duke Ding into decisions he might later regret. Though the leader of the Jisun clan expressed some small remorse at having caused Confucius's resignation, the dancing girls stayed, and Confucius left.

5
EXILE

'At sixty, I listened to what was right.' Analects II, 3

Confucius said: 'It is a pleasure to learn, and to put your learning to its appropriate use. It is a delight to receive friends from afar. It is a quality of the true of heart that they do not care they are not famous.' These are the words that begin the very first chapter of *The Analects*. They are one of his most famous quotes, and are often cited by Chinese hosts hoping to make guests feel welcome, even today. They are also likely to have their origin in the period after Confucius's fall from grace, when he was forced to wander from kingdom to kingdom, peddling his advisory services – not a statement by a generous host, but a plea by an itinerant guest. According to the biography of Confucius in Sima Qian's *Grand Scribe's Records*, it was only in his sixties that he attained anything like the sage-like qualities with which he is associated by later tradition. Until then, he was in the words of two Confucian scholars: 'a sanctimonious and arrogant know-it-all, apt to hector rulers... and to condescend to contemporaries... It is only in his sixties, with his ambitions dashed, did [he] finally become the kind of man Sima Qian could portray as a sage.'[1]

To the south was Song, the state where Confucius's family had fled a blood-feud. To the north was Qi, the state whose intrigues had caused his recent downfall. But westwards, in Wei, Zilu's brother-in-law was a minister with the local government.[2]

When Confucius went to visit the state of Wei, a disciple was his chariot driver.

'There are already so many people here,' said Confucius.

'How would you improve this situation?' asked the disciple.

'I would enrich them,' Confucius replied.

'And after they are rich?'

'Then I would educate them,' said Confucius.[3]

As far as Confucius was concerned, the people of Wei needed a considerable amount of education, because their ruler, Duke Ling, was such a wastrel. Confucius had once openly said that Wei's ruler was only kept in power by the diligence of his ministers since he himself was dissolute and unfit to rule.[4]

Nevertheless, Confucius's fame preceded him. At the border of Wei, a local warden commiserated with the jobless philosophers. Clearly a fan of Confucius's teachings, the warden introduced himself to the travellers, and told them to hang onto their dignity.

'The world under Heaven has long been devoid of principle,' he said, 'but Heaven will use your Master like a bell uses its tongue.'[5] They were kind words for an exile, and as Confucius was to discover within Wei itself, the border warden was not his only supporter.

The travellers stayed with Zilu's brother-in-law for a brief period before their presence became known to Duke Ling. He asked his assistants what kind of salary Confucius had drawn in Lu, and upon being told that Confucius received sixty thousand measures of grain, approved the same sum for him again, leading to a brief spell as an adviser.[6]

Wei, however, was not a good place for Confucius. His attitude soon made him new enemies, and after ten months he found his position souring at court. It is unlikely that Confucius, the stickler for propriety would make many friends in a place like Wei, particularly considering his open criticism of the state in earlier times. He soon made enemies who were prepared to bad-mouth him to the local ruler, who was now in a difficult posi-tion, unable to fire the man he had so publicly hired and praised.[7] Instead, someone (the list of suspects is *uniquely* short) hired local hitmen to make the problem go away. Evading an armed assault on his lodgings, Confucius left the country, but found himself in even greater danger at a border region that had suffered greatly during Yang Hu's tenure. Even though Confucius and Yang Hu had been bitter rivals, Confucius was mistaken for his old enemy and had to run from an angry mob.[8] He was arrested and held prisoner for ten days, until Yan Hui arrived to retrieve him.

Upon seeing his favourite disciple, Confucius was palpably relieved.

'I thought you were dead,' he said.

'Master,' came the reply. 'How could I die while you are yet living?'[9]

On his return to Wei, things actually got worse. In 494 BC, Duke Ling took as his wife Nanzi, a woman who was conducting a public affair with her own brother. To Confucius's astonish-ment, the incestuous relative was permitted to reside at court with the newlyweds and the bizarre relationship was infamous throughout the land, where even the local peasants knew bawdy songs about it.[10]

Pursuing a policy of staying out of trouble, Confucius did his best to abstain from any public association with the couple, who were transgressing fundamental rules of propriety. However, the Lady Nanzi forced his hand by sending him a message, pointing out that it was considered polite for illustrious guests of her hus-band to also visit her and pay their respects.

Tempers were clearly getting frayed in Confucius's circle of disciples. After years of good-natured argument and bickering,

Zilu was scandalised to discover that Confucius was going to visit Lady Nanzi. As far as Confucius was concerned, he had no choice in the matter and was obliged to obey the summons – by his rules, his duty to Nanzi as a duchess outweighed his duty to admonish her by refusing.

'If I have done wrong, let Heaven be my judge,' he snapped.[11]

A messenger arrived from another country, inviting Confucius to visit a local warlord. Confucius saw it as a chance to put some of his theories to the test, but he was restrained by one of his eldest disciples, the obstreperous Zilu, who quoted his own words back at him.

'Master,' he said, 'formerly I have heard you say that a gentleman does not associate with those who choose to do evil.'[12] Zilu argued that Confucius would be betraying his own teachings if he was prepared to lower himself to consort with a man who had betrayed the very same protocols that Confucius valued so highly. The inclusion of the incident in *The Analects* shows how desperate the situation must have become, with Confucius openly contemplating a compromise, and having to be talked out of it by his disciple. Zilu may have been the butt of many jokes in *The Analects*, but on this occasion, he was the one in the right, and Confucius knew it.

Another incident reported in *The Analects* may also have its origins in this exile period, with neither Confucius nor his disciples holding out much hope of future promotion.

Confucius said to his disciples: 'I am old, and soon will be of no further use. Many times I have heard you complain that nobody respects you. If some ruler *did* appreciate you and grant you employment, what would you do?'

Zilu was quick to reply, with a suitably martial response. 'I would like a nation with ten thousand chariots, under attack from several other countries, struck by a blight on its corn and a shortage of its other crops. It could be handed to me, and within three years, I would make its people bold and true of heart.'

Confucius smiled and asked the same question of Ran Qiu.

He replied: 'I would want an area of sixty, no, seventy leagues on each side. Within three years, I could bring prosperity to the people. But I am no good at religious services or music, so someone else would have to do that.'

Confucius asked the same question of Gongxi Hua.

Gongxi Hua replied: 'I would like to help out at the temple services to the ancestors, and at the meetings of the king and his lords. Though I do not know how, I would be happy to learn.'

All three disciples had, in their own way, expressed a wish for political power, in one of the three ministries of Lu – Military, Civil and Public. Confucius turned to Zeng Xi, who was playing the zither at the time.

'I am not so ambitious,' said Zeng Xi, standing up.

'That does not matter,' said Confucius. 'I still wish to hear your thoughts.'

'In that case,' said Zeng Xi, 'I'd quite like a day out. My friends and I, dressed in spring finery, could take some of the boys swimming in the river, enjoy the breeze up at the Rain Altar, and come home singing.'

Heaving a sigh, Confucius said: 'Zeng Xi has my vote.'[13]

While Confucius and his disciples sunk further into penury, their absence from Lu did not go unnoticed. Duke Ding died in 494 BC, and was succeeded by his son, Duke Ai (r.494–468 BC).[14] The administration of this new ruler was regarded by many as unexceptional and poorly managed, a fact alluded to obliquely in *The Analects* when his musicians all began quitting. Confucius had previously been proud of rectifying the music of Lu, ensuring that all state meals came accompanied by the correct tunes and songs. Now, as a signifier of the disenchantment of the palace staff, even the band was drifting away to other commissions.

In something of a shock move, the band-master from the 'fourth meal' – the evening entertainer – left to take up a job in Qin, a western state that was barely considered as anything more than a cluster of illiterate barbarians.[15]

The leader of the Jisun clan sensed that his own end was near, and confessed to his heir that the country would be faring much better if Confucius had not left. It was a little late, but it was an admission that Confucius had been right to take such a drastic stand over the intrigues of Qi. As his health faded, the leader of the Jisun clan commanded his heir to make a revolutionary promise – to reinstate Confucius.[16]

However, such intentions did not long survive their creator. When the noble's son became the new prime minister of Lu, he began making plans to offer Confucius his old job, only to face opposition from other members of his government. The new prime minister was reminded that Confucius had already worked for Lu once before, and embarrassed the state with his resignation. If he were invited back again, only to resign again, it would be a further cause for public ridicule.

Consequently, the government of Lu decided to hedge their bets by offering a post to a *Confucian*, but not to Confucius himself. Bitterly, Confucius sent Ran Qiu off to fulfil the post and continued on his journey.

'Let *me* return,' he said, to no avail.[17]

The disciple Zigong, however, made sure to take the departing Ran Qiu aside and tell him the obvious – that if at all possible, he should attempt to have his Master reinstated in Lu.[18]

Confucius's travels took him to the large southern state of Chu, where a local potentate asked Zilu to describe his teacher. Zilu hesitated, but Confucius later said to him: 'You should have said I was just a normal man, who so loves the pursuit of knowledge, that its pursuit makes me forget to eat, and its attainment brings me joy, such that I forget my years.'[19]

While in Chu, Confucius supposedly witnessed an incident that he would later cite in his discussions of virtue – a group of piglets attempting to suckle from their dead mother, drifting away when they failed to get any milk. 'What they had loved in their mother,' he observed, 'was not her body, but what animated her body.'[20] Material things, he noted, were useless without the spirit that animated them and the context that made them useful.

Confucius encountered a famous 'madman' in Chu (possibly a garbled reference to a court jester), who taunted him by singing a song outside the gate of his lodgings: 'O Phoenix, O Phoenix, how your virtue has fallen / You cannot know the future / You cannot return to the past ... All know the advantage of being useful / But no one knows the advantage of being useless.'[21]

If the local joker hoped to persuade Confucius to stop trying so hard, he failed. Confucius continued his wanderings, even approaching the border of Song, the ancestral home of his family, where he met with the most unwelcoming reception of his career. Confucius and his disciples were performing sacrificial rites beneath a large tree when they were disturbed by a group of men sent by a jealous minister. Supposedly, the minister had been discredited at the Song court by a Confucian scholar, and was determined to avenge himself on the architect of his demise. Local toughs were sent to pull the tree down with Confucius still under it, and the disciples were forced to scatter.

That, at least, is how Confucius's disciples remembered the incident. One of his later critics, Zhuangzi, would describe it differently, suggesting that the vagrant Confucius and his followers had appropriated sacred effigies to use as shelter, and were chased away by angry natives.[22]

Zigong reached safety first, and spent an anguished few days in the state of Zheng, waiting to hear news of his master. Eventually, a messenger arrived to report a bedraggled visitor at the city gates, imposingly tall, but with the general appearance of a stray dog. When Confucius heard the description of himself, he laughed.[23]

The itinerant scholars eventually made their way even further south, to Chen, where they spent a year at the local court. There, Confucius impressed a local ruler, who demanded to know who had killed a falcon on his land. The falcon in question had been shot with a strange arrow – eighteen inches long and tipped with flint. Confucius correctly identified the arrow as a Jurchen weapon, made by a tribe far to the north of the northernmost state of China. He went on to tell the story of the Martial King of the early Zhou dynasty, who had established contact with many outlying tribes, and demanded gifts from them. The Jurchens had sent such arrows as part of their tribute, and the arrows had eventually formed part of the dowry of the king's eldest daughter. Her husband, the current duke's ancestor, had also received the state of Chen itself as his wedding present. It was a moment of Holmesian deduction, as Confucius solved an apparent mystery, not by hunting and tracking down the falcon's killer, instead locating him with the aid of nothing but a good grasp of history. Sure enough, the duke found other Jurchen arrows in his own armoury. The falcon had been shot by one of his own nobles – perhaps even the duke himself, seeking to test Confucius.[24]

Despite such feats, Confucius did not linger much longer in Chen. The state was attacked by three neighbours during his sojourn there, and he had no desire to outstay his welcome. Accordingly, he continued further to the south-west, until he arrived in Cai, a tiny ally of the much larger state of Chu.

The journey marked perhaps the lowest point of Confucius's travels, as he and his disciples idled away the long hours with wish-lists of what they would like in an ideal world.

Zilu said to Confucius: 'I wish I had chariots, horses and clothes of light fur, for if I did, I would share them with my friends, and not complain if they wasted them.'

'If my wish for success were granted,' said Yan Hui, 'I would not boast of my ability, or make a show of my achievements.'

'But what of you, great Master?' said Zilu. 'What do you wish for?'

Confucius replied: 'I wish for the elderly to find rest; for friends always to be true to one another, and for the young to be treated with kindness.'[25]

The light-hearted banter eventually ran out, along with their food and water. Hundreds of miles from their homeland, Confucius and his few remaining followers risked dying of starvation. As they limped ever onwards, hoping to find a place to obtain new supplies, Zilu took it particularly hard.

'Is this what the true of heart are supposed to endure?' he said, angrily.

'The true of heart may indeed have to endure such hardships as this,' said Confucius. 'But only the foolish would lose their self-control when it happens."[26]

Eventually, after a few more stops, Confucius and his entourage drifted back to Wei. There, Duke Ling asked Confucius a question on martial matters, leading the sage to archly reply that he knew something about ritual, but not strategy.[27]

Life in Wei grew increasingly messy. Duke Ling's heir, a child of his first wife, had grown increasingly agitated at the behaviour of his stepmother the Lady Nanzi. Eventually, he attempted to have her killed, and when this failed, he was forced into exile. Soon after, Duke Ling died, causing a crisis of succession. With the true heir absent for attempted murder, the rulership passed instead to Duke Ling's grandson, the Excessive Duke.[28] However, the Excessive Duke was immediately opposed by his own father, who returned to the country to claim his own birthright.

Confucius arrived in the middle of this dispute, and was immediately feted by the pretender, who hoped to appeal to his sense of propriety. Confucius, however, refused to get involved in such a tangle – there was no way he was going to publicly support either of the disloyal parties. Consequently, although Zilu had found employment in the Wei government and urged him to do likewise, Confucius went into seclusion once more, leaving a blank of several years in his biography. Presumably, for that time, he returned to his editing and compiling, and took no part in civil affairs.

Occasional emissaries from foreign lands would approach him asking for advice, but Confucius was unable to parley such embassies into a real job. The disciple Zigong suggested that Confucius should make more effort. Perhaps inadvisably, he used a similar analogy to the one that Yang Hu had once employed, asking Confucius if, owning a beautiful piece of jade, he would keep it hidden in a box, or sell it to a connoisseur.

'I would sell it! I would sell it!' said Confucius. 'But first I would need to find a worthy purchaser.'[29]

He even once mused that he should leave the civilised world completely behind, and find a completely barbaric 'state' to manage, if they would have him. He suggested, perhaps only half in jest, that he should live out among the nine barbarian tribes, but his disciples feared he would find it hard to bear the customs of uncultured people. Confucius said: 'For how long would they remained uncultured, if a gentleman were to dwell among them?'[30]

Zigong tried again on another occasion, suggesting that Confucius should make more effort to appease potential employers.

'What if someone is loved by everyone else in their village?' he asked.

'That proves nothing,' replied Confucius.

'What if someone is hated by everyone else in their village?'

'That proves nothing, either,' said Confucius. 'Surely it would be better if someone is loved by all the good people, and hated by all the bad ones.'[31]

Confucius had come to realise that politics was not a popularity contest in a feudal state. No matter how wise or noble his rules and philosophy, he needed the backing of a truly powerful supporter to institute his schemes. Otherwise, his fame proved to be double-edged. Many would welcome him, but few would employ him. Ancient sources imply that Confucius managed to visit almost all of the states that made up ancient China, but never found his ideal employment. Even if a noble respected him enough to offer him a job, other retainers would fear for their own positions, afraid Confucius's strict protocols would find them wanting.

By 484 BC, his position in Wei was becoming untenable once more. A nobleman came to see Confucius, and demanded to consult him on his plans for a military campaign. Confucius, as was his wont, refused, but the conversation seems to have become quite heated. Harsh words, it would appear, were said about Confucius's émigré status in Wei.

Eventually, Confucius climbed into his chariot and prepared to leave for good, angrily informing his inquisitor: 'The bird chooses its tree! The tree does not choose the bird!'[32]

Confucius, however, had little idea of where he could go next, having exhausted the hospitality of every other state in the region. He had burned all of his bridges, either through telling people unwelcome truths, or simply because others feared him. The state of Chu, for example, employed Confucian scholars in all three of its ministries, but refused to offer him a post, for fear that his personal connection to the other officers would tempt him to lead a coup and make *himself* duke.

It was, therefore, convenient that a messenger chose that moment to arrive from Confucius's home state of Lu. He bore a letter from the disciple Ran Qiu, who had been serving there for some years as a minister. Ran Qiu announced that all was well in Lu, and that the ruling clans were impressed with his institution of Confucian reforms. All was forgiven; if Confucius wished, he could return home.[33]

6
SAGE

'At seventy, I could do as I chose, knowing I would not do wrong.' Analects II, 3

Confucius was now nearing seventy, and had spent many years in exile. His later years found him treated with guarded respect by a generation of new nobles that employed his former students. But Confucius's latter days were bittersweet, tinged with tragedy, a sense of a wasted years and a genuine fear that all he had accomplished would die with him. If we are to believe contemporary sources, Confucius believed that of all his pupils, only Yan Hui had internalised his teachings in their entirety. The others were still picking and choosing – *The Book of History, Book of Songs, Book of Rites* and *Book of Music* were slowly extending their influence, but Confucius knew that many other elements of his philosophy might not survive him. Consequently, he began a final major project, the compilation of an extensive history of the state of Lu, designed to point out the many mistakes of his predecessors, in the hope that later generations would not repeat them.

The Spring and Autumn Annals appears on the surface to be a simple list of events in Lu and its fellow states. That is, after all, what an annal is supposed to be, and 'spring and autumn', in the time of Confucius, was a poetic term for the passing of the seasons.

But over the generations, Chinese commentators have come to impart the annals' every single word with significance, arguing that their compiler (presumably Confucius, although there is no proof) was determined to assemble his history with meticulous precision. Entire commentaries sprang up, book-length analyses picking apart every sentence and looking for hidden meaning in the most simple of phrases and even in the events that the annals choose to record or omit. *Why does the author say 'battle' instead of 'war'?* Because the conflict was indecisive at this point. *Why is the death of such-and-such a Duke recorded?* Because the state of Lu sent a representative to the funeral. *Why bother to mention mynah birds nesting in 517 BC?* Because they are not native to Lu, and may indicate odd weather conditions elsewhere.

Commentators and critics pay particular attention in the *Annals* to their treatment of the years of Confucius's own life, where he found plenty of scores to settle. An entry for 504 BC appears to misname a member of the Zhongsun clan, but this cannot be an error, for Confucius did not make errors. Instead, he is passive-aggressively using one of the two names that a clansmen used for himself, to indicate his disapproval of such a practice.

A 'proper' sacrifice is made in 502 BC, neatly implying that, until Confucius and his followers returned to Lu, correct protocols were few and far between. In 500 BC, men of Qi are recorded peacefully reoccupying borderlands previously in dispute, as a result of Confucius's peaceful policies. In 495 BC, it is recorded that the ox intended for the Environs Sacrifice had been bitten all over by rats – a dreadful suggestion of incompetence on the part of the priesthood, but exactly the sort of thing Confucius might be expected to enjoy noting after his resignation.[1]

The Spring and Autumn Annals dispassionately record the intrigues of Lu but were still regarded by many later generations as a reasonable indicator of the opinions of their alleged author – whoever wrote the book demonstrated a great desire to impugn unsuitable government while praising overlooked ministers. Confucius had reason to feel overlooked. *The Analects* records several incidents when he was harangued by hecklers, including one late in his life when a local yokel taunted him about his celebrity.

'Confucius is great indeed,' said the man, 'but though he knows much about many things, he does not attempt to become famous for anything in particular.'

'Perhaps I should take up chariot-driving?' said Confucius sarcastically, since this might impress his critic more. 'Archery, maybe? No, chariot-driving.'[2]

Confucius was also understandably bitter about Ran Qiu. Although pleased that many of his disciples had found employment in other states, he did not always agree with their decisions. Ran Qiu annoyed him the most, since he essentially had the post that Confucius had once held himself. The former disciple added insult to injury by actively seeking Confucius's advice on a matter of taxation, and then ignoring it.

Confucius was incensed, and wished for someone to arrest Ran Qiu like a common criminal.

'He is no disciple of mine!' said Confucius. 'Children, beat the drum and assail him!'[3]

One of the Jisun clan once asked Confucius to discuss great ministers, a subject which Confucius enjoyed. Consequently, the Master was somewhat put out when the clansman used Zilu, still serving in Wei, and Ran Qiu as his examples.

'I'm sorry,' Confucius said. 'I thought you wanted to talk about *great* ministers, but instead you want to talk about those two? To become a truly great minister, one must serve his ruler according to what is right, and if unable to do so, he must retire.' The pointed reference to his own earlier resignation was obvious. 'Those two, however, they are merely *reasonable* ministers.'

'They will always obey their chief?' the clansman asked.

'Not if he was planning a revolution,' said Confucius, who suspected that the clansman was.[4]

Confucius had trouble adjusting to the fact that his disciples now held the posts that he had once wanted for himself. He was particularly annoyed when he tried to query one of Zilu's decisions, and was told to back off. Back in Wei, Zilu had recommended the disciple Zigao for a position as a country magistrate.

'You are spoiling that boy,' protested Confucius. 'You are forcing him to take office before he has acquired any learning.'

Zilu, however, saw no need to waste any time teaching the appointee about court protocol, when he was eminently qualified to do the limited task at hand.

'The region already has common people and civil servants,' he said. 'It has altars to the spirits of land and grain. Reading more books won't make him a better administrator.'

'This is why,' Confucius replied, 'I cannot stand your facetious cronies.'[5]

The servant had become the master, and Confucius was forced to watch as Zilu made further decisions of which he disapproved.

Thanks to asides in *The Spring and Autumn Annals*, we know that although Confucius was welcomed in Lu, and occasionally had the ear of the respectful Duke Ai, he had no official post. Instead, he busied himself with his writing and teaching, and developed a new interest in a work he had previously ignored – *The Book of Changes*, or *Yijing*. More commonly known in English today as the *I Ching*, *The Book of Changes* was already many centuries old in Confucius's time. It contained commentaries on sixty-four magical hexagrams, each providing an oracular answer steeped in mysticism. Court diviners would ask a question, and then select one of the sixty-four answers at random, interpreting its vagaries to reach an acceptable conclusion.

Supposedly, Confucius spent so much time poring over the manuscript that he wore out the leather thongs that held the bamboo strips together on three occasions.[6] Such interest was a great surprise to his disciples, who had heard him hector them many times about the follies of superstition.

Zigong said to him: 'Master, long ago, you told us that an interest in spiritualism displayed a loss of virtue, and that a desire to know the future led to divination. I took your words to heart, and endeavoured to follow them. But now you are older, and you take delight in these things. Why?'

'The words of a gentleman are as precise in meaning as carpentry,' said Confucius. 'I do not wish to see the future, merely the words of wisdom in the commentary itself. I read *The Book of Changes* for its essential truth, and for its wisdom of olden times. I do not use it to tell the future.'[7]

Confucius's academic interest in *The Book of Changes* may have been genuine, because he retained his former attitude towards other superstitions. *The Analects* reports an encounter between the aging Confucius and an old friend of his, who had found solace in the contemplation of Daoism. Instead of paying his respect to a sage in meditation, Confucius accused him of 'squatting on his heels like a barbarian'.

'When you were young,' he said, 'you were arrogant and uncouth. When you became a man, you accomplished nothing of merit. Now you are old, you refuse to die. You are a pest.' And with that, Confucius hit him on the leg with his stick.[8]

If we are to believe that Confucius was the editor of *The Book of Rites*, then by his own rules, he was due for retirement. *The Book of Rites* clearly states that an official in his seventies should be readily delegating, although reading between the lines, it also offers the possibility that some officers were too valuable to put out to pasture. 'A great officer in his seventies should resign his duties,' says *The Book of Rites*.

'If not permitted to resign, he should be allowed a walking stick and stool.'[9]

In 481 BC, Confucius was called to consult on a matter of ducal concern. He irritably gathered up his finery and travelled to the western reaches of Lu, doubtless expecting his time to be wasted on another pointless question of superstition or strategy (subjects he refused to discuss), or protocol (on which he was tired of being ignored). Instead, it was a case of taxonomy; a minor noble had captured a strange creature during a hunt, and the wisest man in Lu had been called to identify it.

There is no pictorial representation of the beast in question, nor is there much clue in the ancient accounts as to what it actually may have been. But several accounts are unanimous in what Confucius *thought* it was, and the effect it had on him.

On seeing the captured creature, Confucius began to weep. It was a *qilin*, the legendary beast said to herald the birth of a sage, or the death of one. Tied to its horn, so the story goes, was a frayed piece of ribbon.

'For whom have you come? For whom have you come?' sobbed Confucius. 'My time is over.'[10]

The sighting of the *qilin* is the last incident recorded in *The Spring and Autumn Annals*, which closes with the words: 'It was the year fourteen, in the spring. During a hunt to the west, a *qilin* was captured.'[11]

Confucius's reaction, however, has been interpreted in different ways. For his supporters, it was an omen of his own impending death, recognition that he was the 'throneless king' prophesied in his youth. However, the author of the *Gongyang Commentary* on the *Annals* has a different idea, and interprets his weeping as tears of joy; his 'time was over' because all his efforts were about to come to fruition, with the arrival of a true sage-ruler. If that were truly his belief, he would live to see his hopes dashed.

Before long he was taken ill with a disease serious enough to lead to a courtesy call from Duke Ai. On hearing that his over-lord was coming to visit, Confucius insisted on dressing himself in his court regalia as a mark of respect. He eventually received the Duke in his full finery, lying on his bed with his head facing East, as protocol dictated.[12]

Confucius recovered from his ailment, but became increasingly haunted by signs of death and decay. *The Book of Rites* recounts an incident in which Confucius asks Zigong to dispose of his dead dog – an incident in which he muses absent-mindedly about propriety, while trying to hide his sense of loss.

'I have heard,' he said, 'that a worn-out curtain should not be thrown away, but may be used to bury a horse in; and that a worn-out umbrella should not be thrown away, but may be used to bury a dog in. I am poor and have no umbrella. In putting the dog into the grave, you can use my mat; and do not let its head get buried in the earth.'[13] It is an oddly tender, yet somehow doddery moment, as if Confucius is overcome by sadness but still stumbling to do the right thing.

Meanwhile, Confucius became a grandfather, with the birth of a son to Top Fish and his wife. The boy eventually became known as the philosopher Zisi, following in his grandfather's footsteps. He would not, however, know his father, because Top Fish died that year at a relatively young age. True to the rules he had drawn up himself, Confucius refused to give his son an ostentatious funeral, insisting instead on a humble coffin and simple rites.

News came of unrest in Wei, where two of Confucius's disciples were still working as ministers. Confucius ruefully predicted that Zigao would escape with his life, but that the argumentative Zilu would meet with his death.[14]

Sure enough, later reports indicated that Zilu was dead. The scandal-ridden rulers of Wei had entered another round of intrigues, resulting in the current ruler's widowed sister urging her servant-lover to organise a palace coup on behalf of a banished heir. True to his Confucian training, Zilu did not desert the incumbent Duke, but instead began making arrangements to escort him out of harm, into exile in Lu if necessary. His fellow Confucian Zigao advised him to flee, but Zilu continued to act in his lord's interest, and was mortally wounded during a fight in the palace. Contemporary sources report his last words, a lament that he was not attired in the proper manner.[15]

Confucius wept for the passing of his sparring partner of many decades, but nothing could have prepared him for an even greater bereavement that was to follow. Yan Hui, his favourite disciple, fell sick and died. He was barely in his thirties, and Confucius took his death harder than that of anyone else, including his own son.

'Alas! Heaven is destroying me! Heaven is destroying me!' Confucius said, mourning Yan Hui to such a great extent, that other disciples asked him if he was not overreacting.

'Overreacting!' he said. 'If I do not mourn bitterly for this man, for whom should I mourn?'

The disciples decided to give Yan Hui a great funeral, but Confucius forbade them from doing so. Nevertheless, the disciples disobeyed him and buried Yan Hui in style, much to Confucius's anger.

'Yan Hui treated me as his father, yet I have not been able to treat him as if he were my son,' said Confucius, referring to the modest funeral arrangements made for Top Fish. 'It is you, my disciples, who have failed us both.'[16]

Confucius was now convinced that his life's work would die with him, and that his many attempts to educate future generations would be diluted within a few generations.

'No one compared to Yan Hui,' Confucius said. 'A handful of rice to eat, nothing but water to drink, and living in a squalid area would have been unbearable for most, but such conditions never had any effect on his cheerful nature. No one compared.'[17]

In late spring 479 BC, Confucius fell ill again. The disciple Zigong, who seems to have become his attendant in his twilight years, found him hobbling on his staff near his door, quoting an ominous song:

> Mount Tai crumbles
> The great beam breaks
> The wise man withers away[18]

Confucius had dreamed that he was sitting between two pillars with offerings before him – a vision that could only have made sense to a master of protocol. Although the imagery meant nothing in modern times, during the ancient Shang dynasty, from which Confucius claimed distaff descent, it was the prescribed means of laying out a corpse at a funeral service.

Confucius already felt ill again, and he took to his bed once more. His last recorded words were bitter and doleful: 'No intelligent monarch arises; there is not one in the world that will make me his master. My time has come to die.'[19]

Within a week, Confucius was dead.

He was buried north of Lu's capital, in what is now the town of Qufu, and Duke Ai insisted on delivering a eulogy.

'For now, Heaven will not relinquish our retired former minister,' he said. 'Let him watch over me now, as I am a man alone in a position of command. With his departure, I am sick with loneliness. Father Confucius has left us. I have no example to follow.'[20]

Although heartfelt, the Duke's speech angered the surviving scholars of Confucius's academy. They were unimpressed with the Duke's show of emotion, since he had not valued 'Father Confucius' highly enough to give him anything except an honorary post during his lifetime. They were also insulted by the Duke's claim that he was now 'alone', since one of the central points of Confucius's life was to ensure that knowledge was transmitted to others. The Duke's words may have been good-natured hyperbole, but they were not well-received.

7
IDOL

'I make no claim to be a divine sage, nor am I a wise man. You could say that I work without tiring, and I never grow weary of teaching. But that is all.' Analects VII, 33

The disciples went into mourning for the traditionally acceptable period and then went their separate ways, all except for Zigong, who stayed close to Confucius's grave for three further years. Asides in some sources suggest that while they were understandably sorry to see him go, many regarded Confucius at the time simply as a much-admired teacher, and felt no impetus to pass on 'his' teachings. The concept of Confucius as a great sage owes more to the longer term, as some of his former pupils began to lean more heavily on 'the sayings of Confucius', using him as a rhetorical device in their own arguments, and not merely the interpreter of old traditions. Later generations saw the compilation of the sayings of Confucius by his disciples and their inheritors, leading to a growing tradition of scholarship and diplomacy.[1]

There was, inevitably, disagreement among Confucius's disciples as to how his ideas should develop after his death. His follower Zizhang (b.503 BC) tried to change his position on the incompetent, arguing that they should be pitied, rather than ignored. His disciple Qidiao (b.540 BC) tried to argue that some people were born good, and others born evil. Confucius's grandson, Zisi (c.481–402 BC), supposedly wrote the extant classic *The Doctrine of the Mean*, thereby cherry-picking those elements of Confucian philosophy that he found most important, and steering future scholars towards his own biases. Most notably in his own philosophy, Zisi once argued for the inherent *superiority* of scholars, suggesting that the educated man was the better even of his lord.[2]

It was Zisi that would form the strongest conduit for passing on Confucian thought. He had pupils of his own, and one of those became the teacher of the man who is so highly regarded among Confucians that he is often called the Second Sage – Mencius (c.372–289 BC).

Mencius would have a career not too dissimilar from Confucius's own. He served in several administrations, including that of Qi, only to clash with administrators who found his ideas naïve or over-idealistic. Mencius struggled throughout his career against 'the way of a despot', clinging to the Confucian notion that: 'Only the benevolent man is fit to be in a high position. For a cruel man to be in a high position is for him to disseminate his wickedness among the people. When those above have no principles and those below have no laws... then it is good fortune indeed if a state survives.'[3]

Mencius believed that all humans were inherently good, and that the virtues of humaneness, righteousness, propriety and wisdom could all be cultivated and nurtured by the right education. He asserted this in the face of increasing competition from tougher-minded schools that argued for the coercion and discipline of human subjects, and he did so by placing Confucius on an impressive pedestal: 'Ever since man came into this world, there has never been another Confucius.'[4] A Great Sage only arose once every five hundred years, Mencius argued, and the world had missed its chance by never truly acknowledging Confucius's potential while he was alive.

While Mencius saw himself as a direct inheritor of Confucius, so, too did Xunzi (c.314–217 BC), even though Xunzi's approach was radically different. Xunzi read a very different message into *The Spring and Autumn Annals*, seeing it instead as proof that humans were essentially selfish by nature. He did not necessarily regard this as an insurmountable problem, but recommended a form of education and management that steered human beings into channelling their self-interest and competitiveness into useful areas. For Xunzi, humans were born *without* virtues, and needed to be educated into being good people.

Notably, many of Xunzi's anecdotes seem to come from the last decade of Confucius's life, when he had to deal with the disappointing progress of Duke Ai's administration. This seems to help Xunzi present Confucius as somewhat more accommodating and flexible – a man who would rather aspire for better things than give up trying at all, who advises the selection of able candidates, and hopes to mould them into better men. 'It is only when bows are properly strung,' says Xunzi's Confucius, 'does one then seek for the strongest among them.'[5]

We also see Xunzi questioning whether some of the quotes attributed to Confucius were actually spoken by him. In one chapter of his book, he not only argues with a questioner's point, but rejects the entire premise of the question: 'I am afraid that such was not the conduct of the Duke of Zhou, nor were those the words of Confucius.'[6] A century after the death of Confucius, we see the relentlessly rational Xunzi openly challenging statements made in his name, possibly the first historical warning against 'Confucius Says...' fakery.

Presumably, we should assume that when Xunzi told an anecdote about Confucius, the words he placed in his mouth were, at least as far as he believed, things that Confucius had really said. One certainly gets a sense with the Confucius of Xunzi that his character is mostly in keeping with the man we remember from *The Analects*, such as in this pronouncement on having no worries.

> When a gentleman has not yet succeeded, then he takes joy in his ideals, and when he has succeeded, then he takes joy in bringing good order to his affairs. Thus, he has joy to the end of his life, without a single day of worry. As for the petty man, when he has not succeeded, then he worries that he will never succeed, and when he has succeeded, then he worries he will lose it. Thus, he has worry to the end of his life, without a single day of joy.[7]

However, a perfect prince, ready and able to enforce the maxims of a perfect sage, never arose. As in the lifetime of Confucius himself, politically minded courtiers resisted any attempt to bring about enlightened rule through some nebulous idea of simply being good to each other.

The Spring and Autumn Annals would eventually lend their name to the entire era they covered – 722 BC down to the death of Confucius, their supposed compiler. In an alteration of the original meaning, this has come to be known to Chinese historians as the 'Spring and Autumn' period, which gave way to the ominously titled era of the Warring States in 403 BC, the year that one of the major countries of Confucius's era was partitioned and dismantled by its enemies.

Over the next two centuries, the decline of the Zhou dynasty would accelerate. Those same technological and material changes that marked the passage of the Bronze Age to the Iron Age were expanding the capability of states to grow, and to fight for space to grow further. Armies swelled in size, and their attack range increased; boats got bigger, and with them, the ease of moving troops. The patchwork of small states would reform into nine larger polities, which soon fought among themselves. Initially, they would do so within a framework that still paid lip service to the King in Luoyang, hoping for his assent to one of them proclaiming himself a *Ba*, or Hegemon, leader among leaders.[8] Before long, the rulers proclaimed themselves to be kings of independent countries, and instead competed over whose country should take over the King's divine mandate.

Confucius had been a defender of the old order, an order that was already threatened during his lifetime, and which would slide inexorably into collapse after his death. But perhaps even Confucius had failed to see that he was also a product of the very unrest that he despised. The gentleman-scholar, of relatively lowly birth, promoted through merit, arose in his time because the old aristocracy had wiped out so many of its members on the battlefield. The very environment that made a meritocracy possible required the decline of the old system. The prospect of raising low-born officials, or minor nobles to powerful positions might have made sense to Confucius, but it also made sense to many a beleaguered ruler, hoping to undermine the authority of antagonistic noble houses. A gentleman-scholar might regard himself as the best man for the job, but he also arrived in office unable to use his family connections to bring political pressure to bear on the ruler.[9]

The vacuum left by the breakdown of the old ways became the subject of competition not only by followers of Confucius, but by many others – there is talk in the period of 'a Hundred Schools of Thought'. If Confucius was an idol to some, many others saw him as an icon that deserved to be destroyed and discredited. The period saw a number of rival philosophers who, even if they acknowledged his wisdom, were determined to disown him, arguing instead that his worldview was outdated, or that if he had lived in such troubled times, he would have certainly reformed his own ideas.

Among the upstarts determined to challenge him, one of his fiercest critics was Mozi (468–391 BC). Mozi not only regarded many of Confucius's ideas as unworkable in the real world, but as unworkable even in the time of Confucius. Cutting through the breathless prose of *The Analects*, Mozi offered alternative perspectives on many of Confucius's supposed achievements. He argued, for example, that it was rich indeed for Confucius to harp on about the moral high ground, when rumour had it that he let his standards slip if his life was in danger. Mozi pointed to the period of Confucius's exile, when simply thinking virtuous thoughts did not put food on the table. Far from it; Confucius was reduced to eating a broth made from brambles, and, according to Mozi, was soon living a life supported by his disciples' banditry.

> After ten days, Zilu boiled up a pig which Confucius ate without asking where the meat came from. Zilu also divested a man of his robe to exchange for sweet wine which Confucius drank without asking where the liquor came from. Yet when Confucius was received by Duke Ai, he did not sit if the mat was not straight and did not eat what was not cut properly.[10]

For Mozi, Confucius's undeniable knowledge was of little practical value; lauding him for knowing the right songs and the best placements for Zhou-dynasty ritual was like 'counting a person's teeth to determine his wealth'.[11]

The third century BC philosopher Zhuangzi wrote many anecdotes about Confucius, largely clustered around the days he spent in the capital, and the period of his exile in later life. One, however, makes reference to the death of Zilu, implying that it happened shortly before Confucius's own death, and portrays Confucius not as a venerable sage, but as a deluded old man.

In Zhuangzi's parable, Confucius confidently sets out to meet Robber Zhi, a bandit on the Lu borderlands with an entourage of nine thousand men, a fearsome reputation and a penchant for eating human livers. Confucius earnestly tells the warlord that he sees good in him, and that he can authorise territory to be assigned to him if he wants to mend his criminal ways. Robber Zhi, however, calls Confucius a hypocrite and a liar, and demands to know why he is not known as 'Robber Confucius' for the damage he has done to the people around him. Paramount among them is the recently dead Zilu, whom Robber Zhi admired as a swordsman, but who fell in battle trying to live up to Confucian ideals.

> Do you call yourself a scholar of ability, a sage? ... There is no place in the world where you can stay. Your teaching brought misfortunes to Zilu. You have not done any good for yourself or for others. What can be the worth of your doctrines?[12]

Robber Zhi gives Confucius a tongue-lashing that lasts for several pages, and sends him packing, ashen-faced and trembling. His message, common to critics of the Warring States period, is that Confucius is fooling himself by focussing on a nebulous higher purpose, when human life passes as swiftly 'as a horse darting past a crack in a wall'. We might note, however, that even when setting up a possibly fictional Confucius for a dressing-down, Zhuangzi seems only able to do it by threatening him with a sword-wielding cannibal.

Han Feizi (280–233 BC) was similarly dismissive of Confucius's achievements, noting that despite all his pronouncements on virtue and doing good, he only managed to muster seventy disciples in his lifetime. Nor was Han Feizi impressed by Confucius's later tenure in the state of Lu, where, he observed, the real issue was not the righteousness of the 'mediocre' Sorrowful Duke, but his authority. Building upon the rationalism of his teacher Xunzi, Han Feizi believed that coercion would always trump virtue, and Confucius's willingness to play along with Duke Ai rather proved his point for him.

Like Mozi, Han Feizi found Confucius too idealistic. Without denying Confucius's wisdom, he noted that following Confucian ideals would require 'that the ruler rise to the level of Confucius, and that all the ordinary people of the time be like Confucian disciples. Such a policy is bound to fail.'[13]

Han Feizi was one of the early Legalists, a school of hard-line political thinkers. His witty and occasionally sarcastic deconstructions argue for the underlying absurdity of Confucian ideas. He noted, for example, a story in which a man deserts three times from an army on the march, claiming that he needs to be at home to care for his father. Confucius regarded this as filial piety; Han Feizi regarded it as cowardice, and it seems that many of the militarised leaders of the Warring States period would agree with him.[14]

Like Confucius, Han Feizi did not see himself as the founder of a particular school, but merely as the interpreter of ancient traditions. However, Han Feizi and his fellow Legalists were brutally frank in their dismissal of such traditions. People had been trying to make sense of the old books and legends for centuries, protested Han Feizi, and it had got them nowhere. Confucius attempted to return things to the Good Old Days, but he failed. Surely it was time to cast aside the old traditions, and to do what *worked*?

For the Legalists, that meant intimidation. It meant controlling the population through fear and punishment, running states on a military footing, and encouraging a climate of spying on one's neighbours. The ideal Legalist state became an engine of conquest and acquisition, with morals that reflected it – loyalty schemes promising bonuses for service to the state. Criminals could literally buy their way out of punishments, since a fine was considered a reasonable way of reimbursing the state for any misdeeds committed. The prime mover of Legalist thought, Shang Yang (c.390–338 BC), had placed so little value on Confucius that his treatise on power and politics does not even mention him. *The Book of Lord Shang*, however, would eventually become the political blueprint for Qin, the country that would emerge victorious among the Warring States.

Perhaps he was only returning the favour. Confucius, after all, had regarded the state of Qin as little more than a barbarian newcomer, a bunch of horse-rustlers on the western edge of the civilised world. During the tenure of Lord Shang as its chief minister, the Qin state radically reformed on entirely un-Confucian lines, practically under permanent martial law, focussed entirely on a long-term policy of acquisition and aggression. It swallowed up the countries on its borders and bred discontent among its allies. It let the other Warring States exhaust themselves in hardfought conflict, and then swept in to take over. When all was done, the Qin state had conquered all the others, and the King in Luoyang had been quietly dethroned. In 221 BC, the King of Qin proclaimed himself the First Emperor. Before long, he instituted a series of policies designed to lock the patchwork of old states into a single, unified whole. Weights and measures were reformed, the written language was rationalised and countrywide laws were enacted, devoted to the Legalist idea that men were inherently selfish, and required the firm hand of an authoritarian ruler.

This, at least, is how later historians would characterise the rise of the First Emperor and his regime, embodied today by the iconic sight of its famous Terracotta Army. It is all too easy, in hindsight, to write off the short-lived Qin dynasty as some terrible fascist experiment, with grim, unworkable precedents that later regimes would wisely avoid. This is certainly how later regimes would describe it, even if, like the Han dynasty, they actually appropriated many of its institutions and policies.[15]

A more cynical observer might see Confucianism and Legalism as two sides of the same coin. Is it not possible that the very best Legalist might hide his schemes in a feel-good cloak of Confucianism? And might not the pragmatic Confucian speak in public of virtue and kindness, but be prepared to get his hands dirty in back-room deals for the greater good?

It is difficult for us to know, two thousand three hundred years on, precisely how conversations proceeded during the life of the First Emperor, but there are hints that during his early years, scholars still considered the thoughts of Confucius as worthwhile. There are, for example, dozens of references to Confucius in *The Annals of Lü Buwei*, a work commissioned by the King of Qin's chief minister and intended as the ultimate encyclopaedia of all important knowledge. In 239 BC, the book having been completed by his army of compilers and scholars, Lü Buwei provocatively had the entire text of his *Annals* displayed in public, and offered a reward to any man who dared offer a single addition or subtraction to its content. There is, to be sure, a certain arrogant buffoonery to Lü Buwei's behaviour – like many a businessman turned politician, he seemed to think that he could simply buy sophistication by signing his name to the labours of others. But as a reflection of the academic consensus on Confucius some two hundred and forty years after the sage's death, *The Annals of Lü Buwei* is a valuable resource.

Far from attacking Confucius for only attracting seventy followers, *The Annals of Lü Buwei* instead argues that his small number of disciples was a reflection of the dismal spirit of the age in failing to recognise his greatness. But, perhaps reflecting different perspectives among its multiple authors, it also argues that Confucius played a role in the 'greatness' of Duke Ai's administration, a regime derided elsewhere for its poor quality.[16] The Confucius of Lü Buwei's book is also somewhat sharper and more cunning than the Confucius of *The Analects*, noting that: 'To use deception in the face of difficulty is a fit way to repel an enemy. To return from battle and honour the worthy is a fit way to recompense virtue.'[17] The emphasis on virtue is still there, but now it seems subordinated to military tactics – this is not a Confucius that would have been recognised in earlier times.

However, *The Annals of Lü Buwei* would be the high point of support for old traditions in the Qin state. Once China was fully conquered and the King of Qin rebranded as the First Emperor, Lü Buwei himself fell out of favour, and his successors imposed increasingly stricter limits on freedom of thought. The crowning of the First Emperor was increasingly regarded as a Year Zero, before which no precedents, treaties or events should be considered. The First Emperor became increasingly irritated by arguments from his officials that drew on ancient precedents, the traditions of now-defunct states, or matters of religious faith.

In 213 BC, an official protested that the emperor risked offending Heaven by riding rough-shod over centuries of tradition. His comments angered the First Emperor, who subsequently ordered a purge on scholars and scholarship, a prolonged campaign against what he regarded as fake news and alternative facts. It was one of the lowest points in the cultural history of China – an act of brutal philistinism that saw the burning of piles of books and scrolls and the suppression of any text that did not relate to medicine, agriculture or divination. Works that had formed a core part of the Confucian curriculum were taken out of public view, sometimes with only a single copy retained in the First Emperor's library. Some such as *The Book of Music* were essentially lost – only a fragment of this Confucian classic is presumed to remain, now incorporated as a chapter in the extant *Book of Rites*. Some would survive despite the purges; others have come down to us through copies uncovered in graves, but uncountable ancient manuscripts, doubtless including many tales of Confucius, were lost forever, either in the purges of the Qin censor, or in the upheavals that ended the dynasty, in which the capital city and the library of surviving copies were burned down.[18]

Had the Qin dynasty lasted longer than fifteen years, it might have succeeded in wiping out substantially more of the literature that preceded it. But although the Qin state was able to conquer China, it was not able to hold onto it. The empire collapsed within a generation, plunging China into chaos once more. By the time a new regime, the Han dynasty (206 BC–220 AD), gained control, the atrocities of the Qin were seen not as Confucianism's defeat, but as its vindication.

The Han dynasty's adoption of Confucius did not happen overnight. It took sixty years for the reunified empire to establish itself, and for the ruling class to notice that many of the issues that had plagued the Warring States were threatening to return. It was only in the reign of the second Han emperor (r.195–188 BC) that the prohibition on Confucian works was lifted, and appreciation for Confucius began to rise among the administrative class. By the time of the fifth Han emperor (r.180–157 BC), the empire was consolidating further – the old comrades and allies of the founder, previously bought off with outlying dukedoms, were replaced by relatives of the emperor, and served by centrally appointed officials. Confucianism was highly enough regarded by the fifth emperor for the appointment of full-time experts, the Erudites, as consultants on the wisdom to be found in *The Book of History* and *The Book of*

Songs. The sixth Han emperor (r.157–141 BC) continued this policy by appointing an Erudite with responsibility for *The Spring and Autumn Annals*, a scholar called Dong Zhongshu (179–104 BC).[19]

Dong's long career, fraught with vendettas, demotions and promotions, brought him at times close to censure and arrest. Eventually, however, his political skills won through – he survived to become a key figure in the administration of the seventh Han emperor (r.141–87 BC), and proved himself not only in debates with rival scholars, but also in provincial administration and as the tutor of the crown prince. In all things, he cited his understanding of *The Spring and Autumn Annals* as the key to decision-making. It was Dong who would write a memorial to the seventh Han emperor, Wudi, recommending that the administration discard all the 'Hundred Schools' of the pre-imperial days, and follow only the teachings of Confucius, his words as recorded in the likes of *The Analects*, and in what survived of the 'Six Disciplines' – the books of *Changes, Rites, Songs, Music, History* and *The Spring and Autumn Annals*.

'Your servant, in his ignorance,' wrote Dong to the emperor, 'considers that what does not lie within the Six Disciplines and the Arts of Confucius... should not be allowed to be pursued. Only after bad and perverse doctrines are stopped will Your rule be unified, the laws be clarified, and the people know what to follow.'[20]

This memorial has been regarded by many as tantamount to the adoption of 'Confucianism' as a state policy.[21] However, we would be getting a little ahead of ourselves if we accepted that assertion at face value. The Han dynasty was certainly attracted to Confucian ideals, not the least because the age of Warring States was done, and the empire's management now relied more on bureaucracy than military aggression. A philosophy that favoured the training and recruitment of civil servants, and which insisted that such officials knew their place in a state hierarchy, was immensely valuable. It was also beneficial to a nation to have an organising philosophy that emphasised *participation* in the state, rather than the ultimate aim of the Daoists (and, in later dynasties, Buddhists), which in the eyes of a materialist bureaucrat, amounted to tax avoidance.[22]

Nor should we discount the superstitious value that Confucianism could lend to the Han administration. *Somebody* at the court, possibly even Dong himself, had worked out the implications of revisiting the life and works of Confucius five hundred years on. If Confucius truly had been the unicorn-heralded Great Sage, and if *The Spring and Autumn Annals* were a meditation on perfect government, and if it were true, as Mencius had said, that a Great Sage only arose once every five centuries, then the time was at hand for a Great Sage to arise once more. A ruler who accepted the primacy of Confucius, sometime in the 1st century BC, could be the new Great Sage.

There were certainly an awful amount of 'ifs' in this logic, but it afforded the Han administration a degree of smug contentment – Confucius was not merely a philosopher, he was now a prophet who predicted the golden age of Han rule. But to gain the most value from his prophecy, one first needed to accept that Confucius had been the 'throneless king', ignored by his own era. What made the Han dynasty great, it could be argued, was delivering that which Confucius never saw in his own lifetime – a monarch who would accept his words and live by them.[23]

Unsurprisingly, Wudi's reign saw the assembly of some important elements of the Chinese literary canon that might support this belief, including much of *The Grand Scribe's Records*, including its biography of Confucius. It is also likely that *The Analects*, as we know it today, was finalised in that form during the reign of Wudi, possibly even as a gift for the teenage emperor around the time of his coronation. Perhaps it was also rational-ised and edited, with inconvenient or unwelcome sayings thrown out in favour of ideas that would serve the incumbent regime.[24] Wudi, in fact, would also become a keen enthusiast of the hard-line policies of Lord Shang – we might equally argue that his policies were a velvet glove of Confucianism, wrapped around the iron fist of Legalism.[25] As noted above, the 'Six Disciplines' formed a curriculum approved for a Confucian *education*, but even as late as the first century BC, this still amounted to les-sons in traditional government and society. Confucius may have formed an increasingly pivotal role in such materials, but he was still perhaps better regarded as their transmitter rather than their originator.

Dong Zhongshu's masterwork, *Luxuriant Gems of the Spring and Autumn*, is a hefty concordance to the Confucian interpreta-tion of history, which he compiled in the belief that as the work of Confucius in his latter days, it summarised most succinctly his accumulated wisdom. It is difficult to tell today how much of it was really his own work, and how much of it, like the books of Confucius himself, has accreted like limescale over the ensuing centuries as other scholars added their own notes.

It, and books like it, helped steer later generations into regarding Confucius as increasingly instrumental in interpret-ing the traditions of the past, and as a theorist of perfect govern-ment in the present. This, however, did not always go according to plan. An imperial decree in 6 AD made Confucius a duke in the afterlife, but rather than marking his recognition as a state icon, the move was part of a government conspiracy. The emperor who made the decree was only eleven years old at the time, and the honour was really bestowed by the emperor's regent, Wang Mang, a man who hoped to encourage the idea that he was the perfect minister-scholar, perhaps even that long-awaited Great Sage, who deserved to be handed the crown.

By the end of the first century AD, Chinese scholars were sacrificing to Confucius as if he were a deity – Confucius went from being a respected thinker to a legendary figure associated with an accumulated body of tall tales and divine portents.[26] Few works of Chinese philosophy do not take Confucius as their starting point, even if their conclusions oppose everything he said. Confucian scholarship also flourished in other Asian countries, particularly Korea and Japan, where the ideal of the gentleman-scholar became ingrained in the local culture – respect for the old/superior and duty to the young/inferior remains a central element of East Asian culture.

The imperial examination system would come to rely heavily on knowledge of the Confucian classics. Imperial officials had, by default, been expected to know their way around the most highly regarded ancient books, but as the centuries passed, the requirements became increasingly exact. During the Tang dynasty in 681 AD, new applicants for the imperial civil service were required to fill in the blanks on extracts from the Confucian classics, effectively requiring them to memorise them. Six hundred years later, the 'Neo-Confucian' philosopher Zhu Xi (1130–1200 AD) would argue that the books Confucius had supposedly edited were of little modern relevance, and that scholars' time was better invested in reading the 'Four Books' attributed directly to Confucius and Mencius.[27] Although it would not become an official policy until eight years after Zhu Xi's death, this emphasis on *The Analects*, *The Doctrine of the Mean*, *The Great Learning* and *The Book of Mencius* would place Confucius at the centre of Chinese political thought. Zhu Xi's personal commentaries became the default interpretations of Confucian philosophy, and a detailed knowledge of them was mandatory in all imperial examination candidates from 1313 onwards. For anyone who sought to advance through the ranks of imperial officials, for anyone who hoped to become a military officer, a politician, or an administrator, for anyone who sought the traditional Chinese equivalent of a bachelor's degree, master's degree or doctorate, the works of Confucius now formed the core part of the educational curriculum for the next six centuries. And that would become part of the problem.

8
PHANTOM

'Sometimes you must be cruel to be kind. And if you are loyal to your friend, sometimes you cannot avoid criticising.' Analects XIV, 8

Confucius called for a utopian perfection, a return to a mystical age which, if we are to believe existed at all, must also have ended in failure – a decline in virtue that led to the imperfect situation as Confucius found it in his own time. Despite this essential contradiction, later Chinese dynasties accepted that the Confucian way was a noble and worthy cause to which they should aspire.

Zhu Xi and his fellow Neo-Confucians might have updated Confucius, but that only dragged him into the Middle Ages. It was there, unfortunately, that his philosophy would stay, even as the world around it changed. By the nineteenth century, Chinese officials were still being tested on their knowledge of conversations from *The Spring and Autumn Annals*, or the details of harvest festivals from *The Book of Songs*. They would be asked to write essays in which they were expected to follow the approved political line, mounting positive arguments in favour of, say, Zhu Xi's support of Mencius. The wisdom of Confucius, inspired by the dying embers of the Bronze Age, was still the basis of the Chinese school curriculum in the early twentieth century, on the day that the Wright brothers took their first flight.

It was almost entirely useless for the modern world and the crisis China was facing at the hands of foreign imperialism and colonialism. Chinese officials were entering government ignorant of foreign languages. China desperately needed engineers, mathematicians, chemists, pharmacists, medical doctors and teachers of modern subjects. Instead, China's intellectuals were assessed on their ability to write essays on the virtuous ideals of an age of chariots and swords.

Not everybody regarded Confucius as a symbol of unwelcome oppression. The would-be reformer Kang Youwei (1858–1927) argued that the historical Confucius was a revolutionary, not a conservative.[1] Mounting this position required him to claim that he had perceived a dissident message in the classical Confucian canon, and that most of the commentaries written in the intervening two millennia were the work of charlatans. Kang became the willing pawn of the young, reform-minded Guangxu Emperor, instrumental in a short-lived attempt in 1898 to introduce wide-ranging changes. History would have been very different if Guangxu's 'Hundred Days of Reform' had not been so swiftly shut down by the arch-conservative Empress Dowager Cixi, who would keep his imperial patron under house arrest for the rest of his life while Kang fled, Confucius-style, into exile abroad. Kang wanted to repurpose all the Buddhist and Daoist temples in the land as modern, Western-style schools; he wanted to dismantle marriage and the family to create kibbutz-like state institutions and equal rights for women. He advocated a borderless world and, less impressively, the ethnic cleansing of the black and brown races – doomed exercises in social engineering that would nevertheless inspire many later reformers, including Chairman Mao. As part of his brief rise and fall in Chinese politics, Kang also advocated the establishment of his brand of

Confucianism as an official state religion. a 'church' of China to give the modern Chinese a figurehead and an establishment to rival that of Christianity in the west.[2]

Confucius, of course, had no truck with 'superstitions', and would surely have been aghast at his appropriation into a ready-mix state religion. The association with Kang would turn Confucius into a 'religious' throwback in the eyes of some modernisers, although others argued precisely the opposite – that the historical Confucius was a forerunner of the secular humanist movement, and hence the ideal figurehead for modern reforms.

In other words, Confucius was so ingrained into the fabric of Chinese culture that neither conservatives nor radicals could decide whether he was an icon to be praised or an idol to be toppled. He meant whatever people wanted him to mean, in a series of reversals and resurgences that would bring him in and out of fashion for several decades. By the end of the period, he was little more than a phantom.

In her polemic 'On the Revenge of Women' (1907), the writer He-Yin Zhen noted that if Confucius were the spiritual founder of Chinese tradition, he should be held responsible for the crimes of patriarchy and the systemic oppression of Chinese women.

> Consider Confucius, the founder of Confucianism, who was known for discarding his wife. His sons and grandsons learned the same from him. But when it comes to inflicting violence onto wives, the followers of Confucius are truly peerless ... They made it sound as if when Heaven gave birth to humans, men were to be valued and women slighted.[3]

He-Yin held Confucius responsible for the double-standard of traditional gender roles, noting that Chinese women were expected to remain faithful to one man for their entire life, while Chinese men were permitted multiple bed-mates. This, in turn, forced women to accept their roles as either wives or concubines, pitching them against each other as rivals under the same roof. In fact, although He-Yin goes on to give dozens of examples, few of them are from quotes of Confucius himself. Instead, they derive from asides in the books of *Rites* or *Changes* (attributed to Confucius as editor) a comment by Xunzi, and a series of comments and interpretations made by a number of Han dynasty Confucians. A second-wave feminist rebuttal might just as easily argue that Confucius himself had little to say on women's rights, for or against – in the whole early canon of Confucian writings, women are only mentioned twice, in reference to the tense protocols over his encounter with the Lady Nanzi. A *third*-wave feminist rebuttal might argue that this makes their point for them, and that when even Sun Tzu, the author of *The Art of War*, was prepared to take on female students, Confucius accepted none, considered none, and seemed to regard women as beneath his notice. This, in terms of the patriarchal status quo, would make him rather obviously part of the problem, and certainly not a potential solution.[4]

The revolutionary generation wanted nothing to do with Confucius, which was easier said than done. His books had, after all, formed the bedrock of their own education. His most famous sayings were as embedded in Chinese conversation as the coinages of Shakespeare are in English. It was deeply problematic to disentangle the unwanted, hidebound dogma of tradition from the parts of it that seemed like common sense. Were we now going to *disrespect* our parents? Were we now going to *refuse* kindness to others? Were we going to try *not* to be good people?

Lu Xun, one of the leading authors of the radical May Fourth Movement, lampooned Confucius in 'Diary of a Madman' (1918), in which his narrator uncovers a strange journal.

The text was fantastically confused, and entirely undated; it was only differences in inks and styles of handwriting that allowed me to surmise parts of the text were written at different times. Below, I have extracted occasional flashes of coherence, in the hope they may be of use to medical research.[5]

'Diary of a Madman', it is claimed, is the title chosen by the patient himself, after he has been pronounced cured. He had become convinced that he was surrounded by cannibals, and that Chinese society had been feeding on itself for four thousand years, and that only now there was a chance to educate the children into a new way of thinking.

The writer Lin Yutang similarly lampooned Confucius as a pointless throwback in his one-act play *Confucius Saw Duchess Nanzi*, published in 1928 and performed all over China in the years after. The play reconceives the controversial meeting of Confucius with Nanzi, Duchess of Wei, as a series of dialogues. Nanzi, the despised scarlet woman is depicted as a smart, witty, incisive thinker, brimming with ideas and trenchant observations, while Confucius is a sputtering, hidebound, and above all *boring* old man. 'I have lived fifty-six years,' proclaims the Confucius of the play, 'and today, for the first time, I begin to understand the real meaning of art and life... Yes, this is real ceremony, real music...'[6]

Confucius Saw Duchess Nanzi (or in its English translation, *Confucius Saw Nancy*) was a feminist play, carnivalising figures of old tradition – Confucius was recast as clueless, the hated Nanzi as a liberated, vivacious woman, and Zilu, Confucius's disciple, as little more than a thuggish henchman. It relied, however, for much of its impact on the audience's familiarity with the original stories. Confucius takes great joy in the music of Wei, only to be told that it is only better than the other states *because* of the locals' sexual liberation. Nanzi shocks with her wisdom and humour *because* the figure in the history books is painted as little more than a shallow celebrity. And Zilu is funny as a henchman *because* the historical record alludes to his skill with a sword, even as it praises him as a philosopher. Even as Lin's play proclaimed a new era of feminism and freedom, it required an appreciation of the Confucian canon before it made any sense.

Even Chairman Mao, the figurehead of Chinese Communism, grew up steeped in the ideas of the sage he repudiated. Although he called for society to cast aside its traditions and embrace modernity, he seemingly derived his ideals from the fundamentals of Confucianism – a moral compass; a sense of right-thinking; and an emphasis on self-cultivation.[7] In 1920, at the height of the May Fourth Movement to modernise Chinese thought, the twenty-seven-year-old Mao went on a pilgrimage to Confucius's birthplace. In later life, he would rephrase Confucius's concept of the fine, upstanding, virtuous man through a socialist mill – it was the masses who were good, who could make themselves good through Communism. Unlike Confucius, the aim was not harmony, but a constant struggle – a permanent revolution.

Perhaps Mao might have been encouraged to lean a little more on Confucius had not the sage attracted the attentions of his enemy, Chiang Kai-shek, the leader of the Kuomintang nationalists. In 1934, Chiang established his New Life Movement, an ethos of self-cultivation and self-help that seemed to draw in equal parts on Chiang's Methodist faith, his authoritarian leanings, and the philosophy of Confucius. Through concentration on the 'Four Virtues' of a regulated attitude, right conduct, clear discrimination and real self-consciousness, Chiang's movement encouraged betterment through sport, the avoidance of vice, and attention to civic duty in everything from picking up litter to saluting the flag.[8] It promoted frugal living – partly due to the demands of wartime austerity, but also out of a firm belief in Confucian ethics. 'I can find joy in a meal of coarse rice, washed down with water,' Confucius had once said, 'and sleeping with my own bended arm for a pillow. Rather that, than the cloudy illusion of wealth and power, acquired through dishonesty.'[9] Arguably, New Life's cultural high point came in 1940, with the ill-fated release of a *Confucius* movie in war-torn Shanghai. Fei Mu's feature film, which pointedly used the troubled conflicts of the Spring and Autumn period as an allegory for the collapse of imperial China, failed to find an audience in Japanese-occupied Shanghai, and would be lost for several decades before it was recovered and restored by archivists.

The New Life Movement only flourished for a few years, before the concerns of the ongoing war with Japan, and ultimately with Mao's Communists, would cause it to be dropped from Kuomintang political discourse. However, for a fatal period, it meant that Chairman Mao and the Communists came to associate Confucian ethics with their enemies. When the Communists eventually won, pushing the Kuomintang forces into a mass evacuation to the island redoubt of Taiwan, Confucianism would be one of the unwelcome, pre-modern traditions assumed to be leaving the country with them. Confucius, in the eyes of the Marxist-Leninist theorist, was a supporter of the ancient slave-owning society of the Zhou dynasty and a stooge of the ruling class.[10]

Even then, Mao spoke of his mission in Confucian terms. His grand schemes could seem oddly redolent of Confucius's pronouncements at the height of his career about the need for an entire century of the right people in power to achieve a utopia – 'But even if a truly virtuous leader arises, it would still take time – perhaps a whole generation for virtue to prevail.'[11] As his influence waned, Mao came to believe that he faced opposition from 'capitalist roaders' and rightists who would give up on his reforms before they had time to truly take effect. He would die fretting that much of what he had set in motion would be repealed by his successors.

In the spats of 1960s Communism, ancient historical allusions came into play. Mao saw himself as an inheritor of the First Emperor – a benevolent despot, putting China through necessary evils in order to make it stronger and better. His critics were all too happy with the allusion, pointing out that the First Emperor had savagely suppressed freedom of debate and had burned the Confucian classics. Mao retaliated by lumping Confucius in with his most unwelcome rivals. Confucianism, he now proclaimed, was wrong because of its glorification of compromise and harmony – it turned the people into kindly sheep, all bustling to get along with one another. Mao's 'permanent revolution' required constant struggle and confrontation, the very opposite of Confucian harmony.

He initiated the Campaign to Criticise Confucius and Lin Biao, encouraging his followers to write polemics against his discredited former deputy, and, by association, the disgraced sage. Propaganda pictures depicted Confucius as a frail old man, harangued and attacked by the vibrant, earnest youth of Communist China.[12] As Mao's internal tensions with his political rivals turned into a full-blown Cultural Revolution, his Red Guard followers were encouraged to lead a crusade against the 'Four Olds' – Old Customs, Old Culture, Old Habits and Old Ideas. Confucianism, unfortunately, was readily included in all four categories, leading the arrival of a party of Red Guards in Qufu in November 1966. They ransacked the Confucius family temple and vandalised the graveyard, dragging the corpse of one of Confucius's descendants from his grave and hanging it naked from a tree.

The tide of the Red Guards was eventually stopped, and along with it the Cultural Revolution. Mao died in 1976, and his cronies and immediate inheritors were soon ousted. In the aftermath, China began to pursue a new form of state capitalism, shunting aside Mao's utopian ideals in favour of a new era. In words attributed to Deng Xiaoping, the mastermind of China's economic reforms, 'to get rich is glorious'. This seemed a world away from Confucius, who himself said: 'It is difficult to live in poverty without complaining. But it is easy to live in luxury and yet still not be arrogant.'[13] For a while, it must have seemed that neither Communism nor Confucianism had a place in modern China – Mao's feared 'capitalist roaders' were diligently turning China into a surging economic giant.

However, political antipathy was not the only attack on Confucius in recent times. An equally damaging assault on his heritage was arguably undertaken by his own supporters and scholars, as post-modern critics brought their resources to bear upon his literary canon.

The reader may have already noticed that not all elements of the Confucian canon are equal. Just over half of all Confucian materials were assembled in the Han dynasty, several centuries after the death of Confucius, but even those books that date from the Warring States period, closer to his own lifetime, have their doubtful lines. They would have been copied, recopied (perhaps with annotations), lost, conflated, split up and reconstituted. I have seeded some of those problematic areas throughout this biography – although most of the quotes in my first six chapters come from the main Confucian sources, there are several odd moments that reflect contemporary debates about his sayings.

Thanks to digital retrieval and storage methods, modern scholars are able to assemble and assess the sayings of Confucius in ways that former critics would have spent a lifetime trying to muster. At the touch of a button, the modern Confucian critic is able to confirm that Mozi's story of Confucius in the wilderness (see Chapter Seven), relying on his disciples to rob and steal to keep him alive, *only* appears in the work of Mozi. Either there is some earlier, unmentioned source to support it, now lost, or Mozi made the whole thing up a generation after the fact. In the words of the scholar Michael Hunter, 'the author of this passage most likely fabricated a blatantly hypocritical...saying for polemical purposes'.[14] Parts of the Confucian canon, we now have to accept, are probably fake.

We are now also able to check, within moments, connections that might have eluded a scholar without a photographic memory. Take one of my favourite quotes from Confucius: 'Only in winter do the pine and cypress show they are evergreen.' It shows up in *Analects IX*, 27, and is a beautifully evocative statement on making it through life's trials. And yet, a similar phrase can be found buried in the works of at least two other ancient writers, neither of whom bother to say that they are quoting Confucius. Meanwhile, a reference to the 'flourishing of pine and cypress' appears in the penultimate line to a royal hymn in *The Book of Songs* – was Confucius coining a phrase worth quoting for the ages, or was he himself alluding to a song lyric from his era?[15]

Meanwhile, how is it that we can assume Confucius supervised the compilation of *The Book of Rites* in his forties (see Chapter Three) when an entire chapter of the *Rites* comprises conversations between Confucius and Duke Ai, who was not even born until 508 BC? Other chapters plainly depict disciples discussing things that Confucius *had said*, presumably after his death. Either we have somehow misdated the *Rites*, or those chapters are later interpolations. If they were inserted later, does that mean they are forgeries, or simply additions, much as the chapter you are currently reading was added to this book in 2017, thirteen years after the first edition? We know that parts of *The Book of Rites* were assembled later, since two chapters from it are attributed to the pupil Zengsi and Confucius's grandson Zisi, but in which case, why are we bothering to attribute any of it to Confucius himself? How can he be both the compiler *of* and a character *in* the same book?

Similarly, if we accept that Confucius was the editor of *The Book of Changes*, but also that he refused to speak of superstition, then the dating of *The Book of Changes* becomes crucial to our understanding of his developing thought. Even great sages are, of course, allowed to change their minds; the Confucius we wish to study is the philosopher at the peak of his wisdom and the height of his powers, not a callow youth struggling to make sense of a book he doesn't like. Was *The Book of Changes* a traditional scripture that he worked with in his younger days, but discarded as he grew older? Or was it, as implied in *Several Disciples Asked*, a diversion in his later years, appreciated for its wisdom but without any acknowledgement of its supposed prophetic powers?

At least partly, it was such concerns over the trustworthiness of the Confucian canon that led the Neo-Confucians like Zhu Xi to streamline it so drastically in the Middle Ages, cutting it back to the core texts of the Four Books. But even the Four Books, the 'original' Confucian classics, have their problems. Mencius was born a century after the death of Confucius; we only trust him more than other Warring States philosophers because we believe that his teacher was a pupil of Confucius's grandson. Presumably, but only presumably, this gave Mencius special access to family stories. *The Great Learning* and *The Doctrine of the Mean*, as mentioned above, were extracted from *The Book of Rites*, which is already a mess of contending authorships. Maybe it's better if we discount those, too.

Well, at least we can trust *The Analects*... right?

Scholars have been questioning the reliability of *The Analects* since the twelfth century, when the scholar Hu Yin observed that one half of it seemed better organised than the other.[16] In both China and Japan in the seventeenth century, scholars began to suggest that *The Analects* formed, at the very least, two distinct halves, with the 'upper' sections 1–10 being the original version, and the 'lower' sections 11–20 being later additions. Their arguments were rooted in matters of textual criticism, noting that the descriptions of *The Analects* in ancient library catalogues suggested that there were at least two editions with different lengths. *The Analects* as we know it today is largely based on the 'old' text, a copy of which was supposedly found in 154 BC, during the demolition of a building in Qufu, the birthplace of Confucius. But another version somehow survived in what was once the state of Qi, with two additional chapters, now lost – 'Asking About Kingship' and 'Knowing the Way'. Today, we have access to several ancient versions of *The Analects*, including fragments of one from a grave in 300 BC, another that was buried around 55 BC, and another that was carved on a stone stele around 175 AD. But how precisely *The Analects* looked on the day that the First Emperor ordered it destroyed or the teenage Wudi received a copy from his Erudites, we cannot say for sure. We presume that the version found in Qufu was hidden for a reason, and that it might have even been hidden during the First Emperor's purges, but nobody really knows.

The style of writing in *The Analects*, even down to the size of paragraphs, is different between the upper and lower halves. The upper half of the book usually prefaces its quotes with the words 'Confucius said...' whereas the lower half prefers 'The Master said...'.[17] It is almost as if the lower half was assembled some time later, by followers of Confucius, according him a greater deal of respect, and no longer needing to specify who he was.

Some researchers even began to pull apart original sentences. In order to write this biography, I have rearranged the comments and stories in *The Analects* into what appears to be their chronological order. But that is nothing compared to the demolition job undertaken by the scholars Bruce and Taeko Brooks, who have

used textual criticism, changes in vocabulary, contextual references, matters of style and mentions of particular figures to strip
the sayings of Confucius down to almost nothing, and then to
build them back up again. The result was *The Original Analects:
Sayings of Confucius and his Successors* (1998), a ground-breaking
and frankly mind-blowing book that argues almost nothing is
left of the true Confucius. According to Brooks and Brooks, only
Analects IV is likely to contain any actual quotes from the man
himself, and even that is grubby with annotations and additions.
Here, then, is a glimpse of their true Confucius:

> The Master said, He does not worry that he has no posi-
> tion; he worries about whether he is qualified to hold one.
> He does not worry that no one recognises his worth; he
> seeks to become worthy to be recognised ... The gentle-
> man concentrates on right; the little man concentrates
> on advantage.[18]

As for the other nineteen sections of *The Analects*, Brooks and
Brooks claim to be able to place them at particular points in
time – a named disciple asking a question and receiving an
answer was liable to be the author of that particular paragraph,
or at least the person who told that story to a later compiler. Line
by line, Brooks and Brooks build *The Analects* back up, suggesting that the book grew organically, accreting a new chapter every
fourteen years or so over the next two centuries, from the time of
Confucius himself to the day of the fall of the state of Lu.[19]

Duke Ai is referred to by his posthumous name in *Analects
VI*, so either that part was written after his death in 469 BC, or
the version that comes down to us was copied after that date, by
a scribe who respectfully switched out his title. *Analects XVII*
deals with the ethics of serving a usurper – nothing that would
have troubled the state of Lu during the lifetime of Confucius,

but possibly concocted after the conquering state of Chu began interfering in Lu state affairs in 270 BC? *Analects XIX* seems to work as a rebuttal of Xunzi; maybe that means it was written in his lifetime, sometime around 253 BC? And so on.[20]

For Brooks and Brooks, the historical record crumbles when faced with due diligence. They find it suspiciously convenient that so many of the lesser disciples seem to have names relating to minor Warring States, as if later authors tried to make sure that every nation was represented. They even doubt the dates for the birth and death of Confucius, suggesting that they have been shuffled by later chroniclers hoping to relate them to supposed heavenly phenomena, or even that fake eclipses were jammed into Chinese annals in an attempt to generate omens after the fact. They suggest that we are told Confucius died at the age of seventy-two because it is 'numerologically significant', not because he really did.[21]

While the work of Brooks and Brooks is compelling, they have critics of their own. Their arguments require several leaps of faith on the part of their readers, not the least a belief in their idea that the book 'grew' at such a steady and relentless rate, and that everything that currently exists was fabricated over time, and not simply drawn from sources that are now lost. In the words of Michael Hunter: 'If taken seriously, such scepticism may be dispiriting to those who seek direct access to the life and teachings of the greatest sage in the East Asian tradition.'[22] Of course, the post-modern assault on everything our forebears once held to be true is not limited solely to *The Analects*. Similar arguments have been put forward for, among others, the writings of Laozi, for *The Art of War* of Sun Tzu, the works of Shakespeare and the New Testament.

Where does that leave us trying to make sense of a figure that lived and died two and a half millennia ago?

Strict textual criticism, such as has been unleashed on *The Analects*, might leave much of the foundations of Confucianism in historical doubt. It does not, however, make all that much difference to Confucianism itself. Whether Confucius was a real person or an entirely fictional character, the Chinese have been quoting, learning and debating his supposed words for centuries. We can deny the existence of Confucius, if we want to, but we cannot deny the existence of Confucianism. Whoever the author or authors of *The Analects* were, their principles of life and thought, whether they are faithfully set down in 500 BC or made up by some Han dynasty scribe, have formed the bedrock of Chinese culture ever since. In the post-modern era, when everything had been questioned and everything had been denied, when the temples were destroyed and the statues toppled, when the Chinese asked themselves what it actually meant to be Chinese, the question would bring them back to Confucius.

9

INSTITUTION

'Who here does not have the strength to do nothing but good for a whole day? It is possible for everyone.' Analects IV, 6

Taiwan was under martial law from 1949 to 1987. The defeat of Chiang Kai-shek and his Kuomintang forces on the mainland had led to a vast movement of population to the island, which was now and still remains the last bastion of the 'Republic of China'. The huge influx of refugees into what had been a Japanese colony for the preceding fifty years, and one of imperial China's more remote outposts before that, led to the imposition of a one-party state and a tense face-off with the Communist mainland. For decades, the regime on Taiwan would continue to insist that it was the rightful government of all China – a position that would be fatally undermined in the 1970s by increased US rapprochement with the People's Republic.

Putting Chiang's New Life Movement proclamations to an unexpected use, self-styled Neo-Confucians on Taiwan and in Hong Kong began to push for a Confucian revival, hoping to integrate internationalist politics, such as the UN Universal Declaration of Human Rights, into Taiwan's 'Chinese' system. Hoping to encourage the military government to relax its hold on the island and hand over its authority to a meritocracy of intellectuals, the academics Carsun Chang, T'ang Chün-i, Hsu Fukuan, and Mou Zongsan published 'A Manifesto for a Reappraisal of Sinology and Reconstruction of Chinese Culture' (1958).[1] Resting on the New Life Movement's policy of 'cultural construction on a Chinese basis', it called for, among other things, a democratic Taiwan, but also a China that took pride in its own history, and was not obliged to trot obligingly behind the innovators of Western theory and politics. The authors regarded the founding principle of the Chinese Communist Party, which is to say Marxist-Leninism, as a foreign doctrine sure to fail in the long-term, with a poor system of succession that was sure to create unrest, a denial of human individuality and freedom of thought, and a dictatorial leaning that was sure to eventually lead to its own collapse. All of the above led them to search for a better unifying principle. It was, after all, possible to discern a relentless call for rationalism and objectivity in the words of Confucius himself: 'There are people who act without understanding their reasons, but I am not one of them. Hear all evidence, then select what is worthy, then follow that. See much and remember.'[2]

The 'Manifesto' scholars believed that they had found the answer back in the Zhou dynasty, with an ancient ruler's desire that the valued traditions of what was even then the distant past be somehow preserved and honoured by scholar-officials like Confucius. In calling back to the thinkers of China's past, the scholars inevitably turned Confucius into a new icon for modern Chinese thought – and an icon that was compatible with capitalism and prosperity.[3]

Their essay may have had a farther-reaching impact than expected, not in Taiwan, but elsewhere among the overseas Chinese. In Singapore, for example, where a Chinese majority struggled to find common ground for a multicultural society, the People's Action Party came to define itself in Confucian terms as a benign, virtuous elite of scholar-officials.[4] Lee Kuan Yew (1923–2015), Singapore's prime minister for three decades in the latter half of the twentieth century, described Singapore as being 'at the confluence of three great civilisations from Asia, the Confucianist, the Hindu and the Muslim'.[5] Despite the protestations of uncountable scholars throughout history that Confucianism was not a religion, Lee reconceived it as one, thereby neatly skirting issues of race – at least in theory, anyone could become a Confucian. Confucianism, for Lee, was a handy playbook of civil virtues that could be mined to justify his sometimes controversial political decisions. A 1980s policy, for example, aimed at discouraging nuclear families and rehousing grandparents with their children, came with material benefits, tax cuts and concessions, but was cloaked as a return to Confucian values. Lee himself commented that he was 'saddened' that it took legislation and incentives in Singapore before Confucian 'filial obligations' were honoured.[6] But it was plainly a mistake to suggest Confucianism might be a religion. Instead, Lee's deputy prime minister Goh Keng Swee soon described Confucianism in Singapore as 'completely secular' and a form of 'cultural ballast' to be employed against Western pressure. Singapore, thought Goh, could decide on its own policies and ethics, and Confucian scholars would then be drafted in to find something that supported each notion, somewhere in the Confucian canon.[7]

Meanwhile, back in the People's Republic of China, the end of the Cultural Revolution and the fall of Mao's successors had ushered in a new era. The People's Republic of China took over the Chinese seat on the UN Security Council, which had been occupied until 1971 by the 'Republic of China' regime on Taiwan. China began to embrace economic reforms and manufacturing exports, and Deng Xiaoping, the mastermind of China's new modernisation, looked to other Asian powers for inspiration. He hoped to emulate the newfound prosperity of Singapore and

Japan, but also to capitalise on the goodwill of overseas Chinese. It was, Deng hoped, people of Chinese ethnicity in the US and Canada, Australia, Malaysia, Thailand and dozens of other countries, who might be most easily persuaded to invest in Chinese factories and exports. And in the longer term, he hoped to foster among the overseas Chinese a sense that something united them, not only in investment futures, but in some form of shared past. 'By nature, we are similar,' as Confucius once said. 'By nurture, we differ greatly.'[8]

This was not merely a matter of financing, but of politics. The British lease on Hong Kong's New Territories was due to end in 1997, leading the People's Republic to seek some form of common ground with non-Communist Chinese. It was Deng's hope that a successful handover of Hong Kong would allow the Chinese to promote the idea of 'One China, Two Systems' elsewhere in the world – most notably on Taiwan, which might be persuaded to rejoin 'China' as some sort of special administrative zone like Hong Kong.

Confucianism, or at least, the traditional values which it represented, still had a strong hold on China. Despite the decrees of the revolutionary era, one could not simply legislate a Communist utopia into existence. Sons were still expected to perform the filial duty of caring for their elderly parents, an ancient tradition substantially undermined by a One-Child Policy that left a large portion of the Chinese population without any sons at all.

It would seem that the People's Republic of China, like Singapore, hit upon the idea of Confucianism as a handily non-religious assertion of values that would not require saluting a Communist flag or proclaiming one's loyalty to the Kuomintang. 'Be hard on yourself and forgiving to others,' as Confucius once said, 'and people will find it hard not to like you.'[9] There were, to be sure, other possible candidates for a shared Chinese sense of roots, but *qigong* had religious repercussions, martial arts were too diversified and contentious, Buddhism was a foreign import...but Confucianism, particularly when reduced to its ethical components, seemed a lot like simple common sense. It could offer an extremely useful, non-partisan foundation for any dealings with foreigners, and among different kinds of Chinese. Chinese all over the world, including in Hong Kong and on Taiwan, could agree that there were certain shared values that united them, a rational assertion of universal ethics that did not require any acknowledgement of religious faith or 'superstition'. These surely included respect for education, justice, integrity, benevolence and the correct procedures – in other words, the basis of Han-dynasty Confucianism. If the Han dynasty creation of the classical canon was the 'First Wave' of Confucianism, and the medieval rationalisation and reform of that canon was the 'Second Wave' of *Neo*-Confucianism, then the twentieth century saw the beginnings of the 'Third Wave' of *New* Confucianism – the similarity of the names is even confusing for Confucians.

The People's Republic, of course, could not be seen to be adopting Chiang Kai-shek's New Life Movement or the pointedly anti-Communist 'Manifesto' of the overseas Chinese scholars. It therefore needed to publicly rediscover Confucius for itself, beginning with a 1978 conference in Qufu, where academics discussed the culture of Confucianism without fear of repercussions from the establishment that had been resoundingly anti-Confucian only a decade earlier. From 1985, when the People's Republic set up its first Confucian think-tank, Confucianism began to blossom as one of the faces of Chinese soft power. Thanks in part to its association with the Beijing authorities, the Chinese Confucius Research Institute (*Zhonghua Kongzi Yanjiu-suo*) even survived the protests and purges of the Tiananmen Incident in 1989 – after all, it was easy to use the words of Confucius to argue that those student protestors had been failing to observe respect for their elders or use of the correct procedures to bring about social change.

Back in Singapore, similar politicking led to the foundation of an Institute of East Asian Philosophies, which had its day in 1991 when a paper on Singaporean 'Shared Values' attempted to introduce a Confucian-influenced national ideology. While this played well with many members of the Chinese-majority community, other races in Singapore were wary of an attempt to enforce 'Confucian heritage' on them – after all, were we now talking about basic common sense, or were we still talking about something that Lee Kuan Yew had once likened to a religion? The result was eventually watered down, but nevertheless with a series of pronouncements on Shared Values that would have sounded familiar to any Confucian: consensus not conflict, the family as the basic unit of society, respect for the individual, but respect for the needs of society above one's personal preferences.[10] The entire exercise seemed designed to embrace a form of modernisation while still acknowledging a sense of an Asian identity. Singapore's Shared Values now included a 'Confucian' work ethic, whatever that was supposed to mean. Most crucially, such rhetoric offered Singapore, and soon several other Asian countries, a sense that there were long-standing, highly-respected, traditional 'Asian values' that could not be swept aside by the onslaught of Western technology and practises. There was, at least in theory, an Asian way of doing business or an Asian concept of social interaction, and although Asian countries were not necessarily in agreement about what that exactly was, it might have something to do with Confucius.

This 'Third Wave' Confucianism had allowed for the establishment of an international common ground between the vastly different states of the People's Republic of China, the Republic of China, Singapore, Hong Kong, Malaysia and numerous other overseas Chinese communities. It also allowed for all East Asian nations to assert a common sense of ethics that did not need to rest upon the quotations of aphorisms of ancient Greeks or medieval Europeans, a tempting invitation to the likes of South Korea and Japan, both of which asserted Confucian traditions of their own through their long histories of Chinese cultural contacts. And by establishing common roots, there would be other benefits, not the least with the proclamation in 1994 that the birthplace of Confucius in Qufu was a UNESCO World Heritage Site. Confucius was now even helping the Chinese government gain foreign currency through tourist dollars.

In the twenty-first century, Confucianism has adopted many forms. It has become a universal ethical principle guiding many theories of East Asian cooperation and society, but has also been watered down until it is an almost unrecognisable set of fortune-cookie aphorisms. One of its most unlikely proponents was Yu Dan, a Chinese TV personality who used her role as the host of the afternoon talk-show *Lecture Room* to make a series of programmes on Confucianism in 2006. Academics, however, were swift to scoff at her distillation of Confucius into feel-good slogans, and what appeared to be bumbling and basic errors of interpretation.[11]

Yu Dan's biography proclaims that she has a master's degree in classical Chinese literature. If so, either she was not paying attention in class, or she was wilfully misleading the Chinese TV audience when she stated, for example, that Confucius thought the best kind of woman was not a reader of books. Nor was she even consistent in her own interpretations, since a book for her audience was precisely what she next started hawking – *The Analects: Insights*, later translated into English as *Confucius From the Heart*. Despite open attacks by her critics, even in China, on her dumbing-down or possibly simple ignorance of Confucianism, Yu became the primary spokesperson for Confucian thought in the first decade of the twenty-first century, with her book selling three million copies in its first four months, helped along by the bulk-buying of entire print runs by government agencies for distribution in schools and prisons.

Yu Dan's self-help Confucius is a nice warm bath after a long day. He is a breath of fresh air. He is not the stuffy old intellectual of old school books. 'In my view,' observes Yu brightly, 'the wisdom of Confucius does not burn your hands, nor is it icy cold, its temperature is just slightly above body heat, for it is a constant that will remain the same throughout the ages.'[12]

Yu Dan's Confucius is a baffling, rambling text, repetitive and gushing. She stops her occasional speculations about Zhou-dynasty philosophy to mention something she read in an old magazine in her dentist's waiting room about a British tennis player. She quotes something she once heard about the samurai, something she saw on a TV show, and the lessons we can learn from kung fu novels. Hers is, in fact, a book so awful that it becomes fascinating in its own right, but the message it sends, seemingly to millions of readers, is that a Confucian is someone who likes to help other people, who knows their place, who doesn't rock the boat. 'Wherever we are,' she concludes, 'we can let the spiritual power of the ancient classics combine with our contemporary laws and rules, fusing seamlessly together to become an essential component of our lives, to let every one of us build for ourselves a truly worthwhile life. This is surely the ultimate significance of Confucius in our lives today.'[13]

It is critical today, as it has perhaps always been, to separate those who derive true meaning from the works of Confucius from those who see him as a convenient mouthpiece. In that regard, the push for ethical values of the 1958 New Confucian 'Manifesto' may have backfired as everyone, it seems, began to use Confucius for their own ends. The 'Shared Value' concept put into effect by Singapore seems to have found new and fertile ground in China itself, particularly since the call in 2005 by

President Hu Jintao for Chinese people to cooperate in the creation of a 'Harmonious Society' (*hexie shehui*).

This was soon adopted as an official policy, with what had once been a Confucian precept now co-opted repeatedly into government statements. 'Harmony' was now all-important, which perhaps explains the meteoric rise of Yu Dan, since her version of Confucianism amounted to doing what one was told, and keeping one's head down. Yu Dan's Confucian is the ideal citizen of the modern Chinese state, staying happy, non-confrontational, and obedient. Among China's internet users, *hexie* became a sign not of consensus, but of oppression. Dissidents would complain of being 'harmonised', and the buzzword entered social media slang as a jocular homonym – 'river crab' (*hexie*).[14]

If Yu Dan's Confucius were soft and fluffy, then he was also the ideal emissary of soft power. In 2010, the director Hu Mei made a biographical movie about the life of Confucius, starring the Cantonese actor Chow Yun-fat. It was the source of some controversy, originally scheduled to mark the sixtieth anniversary of the People's Republic in 2009, and then pushed back to the following January – a sign perhaps of production overruns, or of factional disagreement over whether it *deserved* to mark a Communist occasion?

The bulk of Hu Mei's previous work had been in television, and her conspicuously worthy epic might have been better suited to an HBO miniseries. Even at two hours, the multi-authored script struggles to cram in all the incidents it deems necessary. If we are to believe rumours that it went through twenty-five drafts, a dozen of them might have been brilliant snapshots of narrower periods in Confucius's life, stapled together to form the final, bloated shooting script. Nestled in the myriad scenes one can see a film yet to be made about Confucius's feud with the Jisun clan in his native state; another about his relationship with his closest disciples, particularly the volatile Zilu and the over-achieving Ran Qiu; still another about his twilight years strewn with tragedy. There were faint shadows of a family drama focussing on his wife (whom he divorced) and children (one of whom married an ex-convict), and whispers offstage of his oddly modern childhood, as the son of an old soldier and a teenage bride, with a disabled older brother.

The spectre of Duchess Nanzi reared up again, when Kong Jian, a descendant of Confucius, publicly complained about scenes depicting the infamous temptress. Portrayed by actress Zhou Xun as a flinty, irascible stateswoman, the film's version of Nanzi is beautiful but unlikeable, educated but capricious, wise but despised, precisely as the sources describe her. However, there is a suggestion, however subtle, that Confucius may have been bewitched by her charms himself, which his descendants could no more abide in 2010 than they could on the release of Lin Yutang's play in 1928.[15]

More troublesome for the film's reception was an apparent desperation to establish its historical authenticity, spattering many a scene with onscreen annotations. The final result, despite occasional high points, ended up feeling less like entertainment and more like homework. As audiences in the People's Republic embarrassingly flocked instead to see James Cameron's *Avatar*, the authorities ordered the assignment of *Confucius* to more screens, essentially in an attempt to force movie-goers to accept it over the Hollywood alternative.[16] If such a decision seems heavy-handed, we should perhaps remember that soft power means something very different to the devout Confucian and the earnest Communist Party official. Confucius the movie producer would surely have called for a better film, suitable to win hearts and minds. The promoters of the *Confucius* movie favoured a more Legalist policy – limiting the choices of the audience until they glumly accepted it.

Since 2004, China's Ministry of Education has expanded its influence abroad through the setting up of 'Confucius Institutes'. The first opened in Seoul, South Korea – today, there are some four hundred and eighty similar institutes operating worldwide. A Confucius Institute operates as an overseas cultural ambassador for the People's Republic of China. It arranges educational programmes and cultural exchanges. Often on university campuses, it serves as a meeting point and social site for Chinese students overseas, whose presence on campus as fee-paying scholars is often a direct result of the Institute's presence.

'The Confucius Institute is an appealing brand for extending our culture abroad,' commented the politician Li Changchun. 'It has made an important contribution towards our soft power. The Confucius brand has a natural attractiveness. Using the excuse of teaching Chinese language, everything looks reasonable and logical.'[17]

What is attractive about the 'brand' of Confucius? Cultural outreach organisations from other countries often attach themselves to the name of some iconic figure – the Germans have their Goethe-Institut, the Spanish have their Instituto Cervantes, but Confucius, a figure worshipped like a deity in a dozen countries, must surely trump them all. It is difficult to conceive of any other Chinese historical figure with worldwide name-recognition. Even *The China Post*, a newspaper in Taiwan, could see the appeal:

Certainly, China would have made little headway if it had named these Mao Institutes, or even Deng Xiaoping Institutes. But by borrowing the name Confucius, it created a brand that was instantly recognised as a symbol of Chinese culture, radically different from the image of the Communist Party.[18]

Perhaps if they *had* named them Mao Institutes, the international community would not be quite so surprised at the level of Party interference behind the scenes. Confucius Institutes bring with them tempting financial incentives, as well as the promise of grants, programmes and activities. Many an academic institution has taken their shilling before truly appreciating the implications – discouragement of any mention of Tibet or Taiwan, no discussion of controversial issues like the Tiananmen Square incident or the suppression of the Falun Gong cult. They might be named for Confucius, but the Confucius Institutes are unquestionably organs of the Chinese Communist Party, an organisation that once called for the destruction of Confucian thought, and that has only embraced him in the last few decades as a convenient international mascot.

In the second decade of the twenty-first century, there was a bizarre spat over the Confucius 'brand' when a committee attempted to set up a Confucius Peace Prize, initially in response to the controversial decision to award the Nobel Peace Prize in 2010 to the dissident Liu Xiaobo. Seemingly with Chinese government collusion, at least at first, a privately-funded initiative proposed the inauguration of a Confucius Peace Prize, challenging the Nobel committee's assumption of the moral high ground by choosing winners that promoted 'world peace from an East Asian Perspective'.

Here, we can perhaps see the faint echoes of the Manifesto scholars' call for an Asian perspective, although the Confucius Peace Prize was probably not what they had in mind. The first was awarded to Lien Chan, a Taiwanese official who had been instrumental in forging ties between Taiwan and mainland China. However, there were already intimations of trouble behind the scenes – the Chinese Ministry of Culture withdrew what little support it had previously offered, and the awards committee itself was split by factionalism. The Confucius Peace Prize was

seemingly dead, only for a splinter group of the original committee to re-form in Hong Kong and proclaim the Prize was still an
ongoing concern. The second Confucius Peace Prize was handed
out to Vladimir Putin. In 2014, after a Japanese politician had
declined the increasingly dubious honour, the golden statue of
Confucius went to Robert Mugabe.

Such an appropriation of the image of Confucius surely does no
good – not even the winners seemed all that willing to collect their
award in person, making the Prize more eager to associate itself
with them than they were to associate themselves with the Prize.
As Confucius said himself: 'There are three types of friends that are
good for you and three that are bad. You benefit from friendship
with those who are upright, loyal and intelligent, but it is harmful
to keep the company of flatterers, hypocrites and the ignorant.'[19]

In the twenty-first century, Confucius has literally become
an institution, although one questions whether many of the officials and committees who currently lay claim to him appreciate
his true message for the ages. Empty ritual disgusted him; what
mattered was that the worshippers meant what they said, and put
it into practice in the world at large.

Two and half thousand years after he lived, and despite the
actions of contemporary carpet-baggers, the words of Confucius
are just as relevant today. His thoughts on always doing the
right thing, on returning the respect of others, and of striving to
improve the lives of everyone with whom we come into contact,
have become fundamental tenets of humanism. Confucius offers
a common ground for modern times, a sacred tradition that values true goodness, and calls for respect and honour in our daily
dealings. Whichever god or gods you believe have set the mystic
Mandate, Confucius calls us all to turn our eyes away from the
distant divine, and look around us at what we can do to make the
world a better place.

CHRONOLOGY

c.551 BC Birth of Confucius. 28 September 551 is commonly accepted as the official date.

c.547 Death of Confucius's father.

c.541 Duke Zhao becomes the ruler of Lu.

c.531 Confucius marries.

c.530 Confucius gains employment as manager of a state granary. Birth of Confucius's son, Li, also known as Boyu, or Top Fish.

c.529 Confucius promoted to state husbandry manager.

c.528 Confucius begins teaching.

c.527 Death of Confucius's mother.

c.520 Confucius meets Duke Jing, ruler of the neighbouring state of Qi.

c.518 Meng-xi of the Mengsun Clan recommends the promotion of Confucius on his death-bed.

c.517 Confucius visits the royal capital, Luoyang and possibly meets Laozi.

c.516 After a conflict breaks out in Lu, Confucius is forced to briefly relocate to Qi.

c.511 Confucius possibly begins compiling *The Book of History* and *The Book of Songs*. Birth of Yan Hui, Confucius's cousin and favourite disciple.

c.510 Death of Duke Zhao in exile. Duke Ding takes over.

c.510 According to some sources, Confucius divorces his wife.

c.510? Confucius allows his daughter to marry Gong Ye-chang.

c.501 Confucius becomes the chief magistrate of Zhong-du.

c.500 Duke Ding makes Confucius assistant to the assistant-superintendent of public works. Confucius's diplomacy at a summit saves his lord's life.

c.499. Confucius becomes Minister of Justice, or 'prime minister'.

c.497 Confucius resigns.

c.496 Confucius heads east to Wei, and then to the border, where he is mistaken for his old enemy Yang Hu.

c.494 Death of Duke Ding. His son, Duke Ai, still a teenager, becomes the new ruler of Lu.

c.493. Death of Duke Ling in Wei.

c.490 Death of the ruler of Qi, Duke Jing.

c.491 Confucius travels to several kingdoms in the region, but is unable to find long-term employment.

c.485 Death of Confucius's wife.

c.484. Returns to Lu after the successes of his disciple Ran Qiu. Presumably begins editing and adapting Lu's state history, *The Spring and Autumn Annals*.

c.483 Death of Confucius's son Top Fish. Supposed birth-date of Confucius's grandson Zisi.

c.481 Confucius aged seventy. The supposed capture of a *qilin* in western Lu is the last entry in *The Spring and Autumn Annals*.

c.479 Death of Zilu during a revolution in Wei. Death of Yan Hui.

c.479 Death of Confucius.

249 Conquest of Lu by the state of Chu.

223 Chu, including what was once Confucius's homeland, is conquered by the state of Qin.

221 Conquest of Qi by the state of Qin – the last independent state to fall. The King of Qin renames himself The First

Emperor. The 'Qi' variant of *The Analects* appears to have survived long enough to gain two additional chapters.

213 The First Emperor of China orders a purge of traditional literature, including the works of Confucius.

206 Collapse of the Qin dynasty.

191 The second emperor of the Han dynasty lifts the ban on Confucian books. Surviving Confucians presumably set down *The Analects* to the best of their memory. The version assembled by scholars from Qi has two extra chapters, now lost.

154 A manuscript of *The Analects* is found during the demolition of an old building in Qufu. It is this version that supposedly forms the basis of *The Analects* as it has come down to us today.

1 AD Pingdi, the eleven-year-old Emperor of Peace, confers ducal rank on Confucius in the afterlife.

6 AD Pingdi is poisoned by his regent, Wang Mang, who attempts to claim the throne proclaiming himself as a Confucian sage. His usurpation lasts until 23 AD before the Han dynasty is restored.

57 AD Imperial colleges begin to offer sacrifices to Confucius.

492 AD During the reign of Wudi, the Martial Emperor, Confucius is conferred with the title 'Accomplished Sage'.

609 AD Confucius becomes the subject of veneration in dedicated temples.

681 AD Applicants for the imperial civil service must fill in the blank spaces on extracts from the Confucian classics, effectively requiring all would-be officials to memorise them.

1208 AD The 'Neo-Confucian' philosophy of Zhu Xi is accepted as the dominant ideology at the court of the Song emperor. Its emphasis is on the 'Four Books' – *The Analects*, *The Great Learning*, *The Doctrine of the Mean*, and the book of Mencius.

1313 AD Zhu Xi's commentaries on the Confucian classics become compulsory subjects in the imperial civil service exams.

1530 AD Jiajing, the Emperor of Admirable Tranquility, names Mencius as 'the Second Sage', officially weaving Mencian thought into the fabric of Confucianism.

1645 AD In a likely attempt to make the Manchu invasion force look more 'Chinese', Shunzhi, the Emperor of Unbroken Rule, proclaims Confucius to be 'the Ancient Teacher, Accomplished and Illustrious, the Perfect Sage'.

1687 AD. Italian Jesuits translate *The Analects* into Latin, Romanising the name Kong Fuzi (Master Kong) as 'Confucius'.

1704 AD Pope Clement XI forbids Chinese Catholics from performing rites in honour of Confucius or their ancestors.

1898 AD. The short-lived Hundred Days' Reform fails to establish Confucianism as the 'church' of China.

1905 AD The imperial civil service examinations suspend the requirement for candidates to know the Four Books of Confucius and Mencius.

1906 AD Guangxu, the Emperor of Shining Sequence, decrees that sacrifice to Confucius should be undertaken at the same level as sacrifice to Heaven and Earth.

1907 AD He-Yin Zhen's essay 'The Revenge of Women' blames Confucius for the double-standard in Chinese gender roles.

1912 AD Abdication of the Last Emperor.

1919 AD The May Fourth Movement demands modernisation. As a symbol of tradition, Confucius is singled out as an outmoded icon.

1928 AD Lin Yutang's play *Confucius Saw Duchess Nanzi* presents the philosopher as a figure of ridicule. The Kong family, his direct descendants, complain that it is a 'public insult'.

1931 AD Lin translates his own play into English as *Confucius Saw Nancy*.

1934 AD Chiang Kai-shek's Confucius-inspired 'New Life' movement makes Mao Zedong wary of Confucian values.

1940 AD Fei Mu's *Confucius* film, which uses his later life as an allegory for the disruption of contemporary China at war, flops on its initial release in Shanghai.

1949 AD Establishment of Communist rule in China. Confucian values are challenged as patriarchal and oppressive.

1958 AD Overseas Chinese scholars publish the 'Manifesto for a Reappraisal of Sinology and the Reconstruction of Chinese Culture', denying Communism and reasserting Confucian values.

1966 AD Red Guards attack the cemetery of Confucius during the Cultural Revolution.

1973 AD The final flourish of the Cultural Revolution includes the 'Criticise Lin Biao, Criticise Confucius' campaign. Three astronomers at the Palomar Observatory christen a newly discovered asteroid 7853 Confucius.

1978 AD Shandong University convenes a symposium on Confucian Studies, part of an ongoing campaign to reclaim and re-examine formerly discredited traditions.

1980 AD Establishment of the Confucius Research Centre in Qufu, Shandong.

1984 AD Mass public celebrations of Confucius's two thousand, five hundred and thirty-fifth birthday suggest the tacit assent of the Communist Party.

1985 AD Foundation of the China Confucius Research Institute in Beijing.

1986 AD Confucian-inspired ideas included in the new Five-Year Plan. Confucianism is now arguably part of Chinese government policy.

1987 AD Joint China-Singapore conference on Confucianism promotes it as the 'cultural force' behind East Asian economic development.

1990 AD Shandong's local TV network produces a sixteen-part TV series about the life of Confucius.

1991 AD Lee Kwan Yew's Singapore positions itself as a nation of 'Shared Values' with a 'Confucian' work ethic.

1994 AD The cemetery of Confucius and his family temple in Qufu are proclaimed a UNESCO world heritage site.

2004 AD Foundation of the first overseas 'Confucius Institute' with the cooperation of the Ministry of Education of the People's Republic of China.

2005 AD Chinese president Hu Jintao calls for a 'Harmonious Society', turning a Confucian precept into a new buzzword.

2006 AD Yu Dan's *The Analects: Insights* sells three million copies in its first four months. The concept of a Harmonious Society is adopted as a Communist Party resolution.

2010 AD A privately run committee awards the first 'Confucius Peace Prize'. Future winners include Vladimir Putin, Fidel Castro and Robert Mugabe. Chinese government support for Hu Mei's *Confucius* biopic leads to a backlash after James Cameron's *Avatar* is dropped from cinemas to make way for it.

2017 AD Confucius's two thousand, five hundred and sixty-eighth birthday. Six million people describe themselves as 'Confucianists'. Another 350 million follow his teachings. There are four hundred and eighty 'Confucius Institutes' worldwide.

CONFUCIUS SAYS...
THE LAST WORD

The first edition of this book came with my own translations of many Confucian sayings scattered in sidebars throughout the text. For this second edition, prepared for an era where they would ruin the layout on e-book pages, I have integrated some of these into the main text. The others are reprinted here.

'It does not bother me that others do not know me, but it bothers me that I do not know others.' ANA I, 16

'A gentleman must be wary of three things. In his youth, before his ardour cools, he must guard against lust. When he becomes a man, and his spirit is strong, he must guard against anger. When he attains old age and his spirit declines, he must guard against greed.' ANA XVI, 7

'There is no need to discuss something that has already been done. There is no gain in scolding for an act that has already finished. There is no point in blaming anyone.' ANA III, 21, iii

'If you wish to do good work, you must first sharpen your tools. Wherever you may live, seek employment with the most worthy citizens, and befriend the most honourable scholars.' ANA XV, 9

'Without dedication, none shall respect you and your studies will suffer. Value faithfulness and sincerity above all other things. Have no friends who are not equal to yourself. When you make a mistake, do not be afraid to make amends.' ANA I, 8

'The virtuous always speak correctly, but merely saying the right thing is no proof of virtue. Heroes may be brave, but not all of those who act bravely are necessarily heroes.' ANA XIV, 5

'Learning is like building. If I am making an earth mound and advance a single bucket at a time, what matters is that I am advancing. But if I stop one bucket away from completion, what matters is that I have stopped.' ANA IX, 18

'There is nothing I can do about those who do not think before they act.' ANA XV, 15

'Ignoring someone worthy of hearing is an insult to them. Speaking to someone unworthy of hearing is an insult to yourself. The truly wise neither lose companions, nor waste their words.' ANA XV, 7

'Be courteous, and you will not be humiliated. Be wide-ranging, and you will gain the love of the people. Be honourable, and others shall trust you. Be diligent, and you shall eventually succeed in every task.' ANA XVII, 6

'If you treat those below you with disdain, you will be in danger. For the true of heart to remain righteous is like climbing a tree. The higher you ascend, the greater the distance you may fall.' SDA, 5

'A gentleman would rescue a man trapped in a well, but he would not jump in himself. He is not perfect, but he is not stupid, either.' ANA VI, 24

'Set your heart upon the true path, support yourself with righteousness, wear goodness upon you, seek distraction in the arts.' ANA VII, 6

'Our ancestors were careful in their speech, for fear that their actions would not support it. The cautious seldom err. The virtuous are slow in words and true in deeds.' ANA II, 33–34

'Gossip and the spreading of rumours runs against the path of true virtue.' ANA XVII, 14

'Matters of depth and importance may be discussed with those who have talent. They should not be debated with those whose talents are mediocre.' ANA VI, 19.

'Do not impose on your ruler, and, moreover, if you must disagree, do so to his face.' ANA XIV, 23

'The true of heart practise before they preach, and speak from experience.' ANA II, 13

'Advise friends loyally and guide them to the best of your ability. If they pay no attention, then stop, or you risk embarrassment.' ANA XII, 23

'The true of heart help others achieve their good wishes. The wicked only help others enact their ill will.' ANA XII, 16

'Righteousness is not so far away. Wish for it to be so, and righteousness shall be by your side.' ANA VII, 29

'Boasts are harder to honour than promises.' ANA XIV, 21

'I have searched in vain for someone who is capable of seeing their own faults, and bringing the charge against themselves.' ANA V, 26

'In judging criminal cases, I am impartial like any other. But surely it is better to have no crimes at all.' ANA XII, 13

'The true of heart are not unyielding, but only unyielding when they are right.' ANA XV, 36

Confucius was asked if the true of heart should act kindly towards their enemies. Confucius said: 'If I did that, how should I act towards my friends? Meet kindness with kindness, but meet resentment with the merit it deserves.' ANA XIV, 34

'You must be serious in daily life, attentive in your work, sincere in your dealings with others. Even though you may walk among barbarians, you should not let such concerns slide.' ANA XIII, 19

'An army can be deprived of its commander, but you cannot be deprived of your will.' ANA IX, 26

Zigong would often sneer at others' shortcomings. Confucius said: 'Are you really so perfect, yourself? I don't have time for this.' ANA XIV, 31

'If you reward the straight over the crooked, they will be obedient. If you reward the crooked over the straight, they will be disgruntled.' ANA II, 19

'The wise do not promote people simply for what they say, nor do they ignore good advice simply because of who says it.' ANA XV, 22

'The best of the wise and the worst of the stupid are only so called so because they cannot be changed.' ANA XVII, 3

'There is more to life than cramming yourself with food all day. Play chess or something. Anything is better than nothing.' ANA XVII, 22

The disciple Yuan Si became an important official, but when Confucius offered him nine hundred measures of grain, he refused. Confucius said: 'Do not refuse. Take them, and give them away amongst the villagers.' ANA VI, 3, iii

'I hope that old people live lives free of cares, that my friends have faith in me, and that the young shall remember me when I am gone.' ANA V, 25, iv

'The foolish speak often, and make many mistakes. They do too much, and cause themselves to worry.' SDA, 13

'The wise pick the right moment. Then they exert all their strength until the task is done, not resting at the noon of day, nor in the twilight of their years.' SDA, 15

'Do not be too fond of drink.' ANA IX, 16

'Those who do not think ahead will soon find their troubles close at hand.' ANA XV, 11

When riding in a carriage, Confucius did not gawp out of the window. Nor did he shout and point. ANA X, 17, ii

REFERENCES AND FURTHER READING

Ariel, Y. *K'ung-ts'ung-tzu – The K'ung Family Masters' Anthology*. Princeton: Princeton University Press, 1989.

Barmé, G (ed.). *China Story Yearbook 2012 – Red Rising, Red Eclipse*. Canberra: Australian National University College of Asia & the Pacific, 2012.

Brooks, E. and Taeko Brooks. *The Original Analects: Sayings of Confucius and his Successors*. New York: Columbia University Press, 1998.

Barnes, G. *The Rise of Civilisation in East Asia: The Archaeology of China, Korea and Japan*. London: Thames & Hudson, 1999.

Chang, C. *A Life of Confucius*. Taipei: Hwakang Press, 1971.

Chen, K. and Hu Zhihui, eds. *Zuo's Commentary*. Changsha: Hunan People's Press, 1997.

Chin, A. *Confucius: A Life of Thought and Politics*. New Haven: Yale University Press, 2008.

Clark, P. *The Chinese Cultural Revolution: A History*. Cambridge: Cambridge University Press, 2008.

Cleary, T. *The Essential Confucius*. New York: Castle Books, 1992.

Clements, J. *Sun Tzu's Art of War – A New Translation*. London: Constable, 2012.

_____. *The First Emperor of China*. 2nd edition. London: Albert Bridge Books, 2015.

_____. *A Brief History of the Martial Arts: East Asian Fighting Styles from Kung Fu to Ninjutsu*. London: Robinson, 2016.

Cotterell, A. *The First Emperor of China*. London: Macmillan, 1981.

Dawson, R. *Confucius*. Oxford: Oxford University Press, 1981.

de Bary, W. and Richard Lufrano (eds). *Sources of Chinese Tradition, Volume Two: From 1600 Through the Twentieth Century*. Second Edition. New York: Columbia University Press, 2000.

Foust, M. and Sor-hoon Tan (eds). *Feminist Encounters with Confucius.* Leiden: E.J. Brill, 2016.

Fu, J., and Chen Songchang. *Mawangdui Han mu wenwu: Cultural Relics Unearthed from the Han Tombs at Mawangdui.* Changsha: Hunan Press, 1992.

Guo, S. *A History of Chinese Confucianism.* Shanghai: Shanghai Foreign Language Education Press, 2010.

Höchsmann, H. and Yang Guorong. *Zhuangzi.* Abingdon: Routledge, 2016.

Hunter, M. *Confucius Beyond the Analects.* Leiden: E.J. Brill, 2017.

Hutton, E. *Xunzi: The Complete Text.* Princeton: Princeton University Press, 2014.

Ikeda, T. 'Maōtei Kan bo hakusho Shūeki Yō hen no Kenkyū' [Researches into the Scroll *Essentials of The Yijing* from the Han Dynasty Tomb at Mawangdui], in *Tōyō Bunka*, 123, pp.111–207, 1994.

Johnston, I. *The Book of Master Mo.* Harmondsworth: Penguin, 2013.

Knoblock, J. and Jeffrey Riegel (eds). *The Annals of Lü Buwei – A Complete Translation and Study.* Stanford: Stanford University Press, 2000.

Kong, D. and Ke Lan. *The House of Confucius.* London: Hodder & Stoughton, 1988.

Kramers, R. *K'ung Tzu Chia Yü: The School Sayings of Confucius [Kongzi Jiayu a.k.a Narratives of the School].* Leiden: E.J. Brill, 1950.

Lau, D. *Mencius.* Revised Edition. Harmondsworth: Penguin, 2004.

Legge, J., ed. (1893) *Confucius: Confucian Analects, The Great Learning and The Doctrine of the Mean, Translated with Critical and Exegetical Notes, Prolegomena, Copious Indexes and Dictionary of All Characters.* New York: Dover (1971 reprint).

_____. *The Works of Mencius.* Oxford: Clarendon Press, 1895.

Lewis, M. *The Early Chinese Empires: Qin and Han.* Cambridge, MA: Harvard University Press, 2007.

Lin, Y. *Confucius Saw Nancy and Essays About Nothing.* Shanghai: The Commercial Press, 1936.

Liu, L. et al. *The Birth of Chinese Feminism: Essential Texts in Transnational Theory.* New York: Weatherhead East Asia Institute, Columbia University, 2013.

Loewe, M. *A Biographical Dictionary of the Qin, Former Han & Xin Periods (221 BC–AD 24).* Leiden: E.J. Brill, 2000.

Lu Xun. *The Story of Ah-Q and Other Tales of China: The Complete Fiction of Lu Xun.* [trans. Julia Lovell]. Harmondsworth: Penguin, 2009.

Luo, C. et al. *Kongzi Mingyan: A Collection of Confucius' Sayings*. Jinan: Qi Lu Press, 1988.

Milburn, O. *The Glory of Yue: An Annotated Translation of the Yuejue Shu*. Leiden: E.J. Brill, 2010.

_____. *The Spring and Autumn Annals of Master Yan*. Leiden: E.J. Brill, 2016.

Miller, H. *The Gongyang Commentary on the Spring and Autumn Annals – A Full Translation*. New York: Palgrave Macmillan, 2015.

Müller, M., ed. (1885) *Sacred Books of China, Vol. III and IV – The Li Ki (Liji – Book of Rites)*, trans. James Legge. Delhi: Motilal Banarsidass (1966 reprint).

Nienhauser, W. (ed.) *The Grand Scribe's Records: Volume I – The Basic Annals of Pre-Han China*. Bloomington: Indiana University Press, 1994.

_____. *The Grand Scribe's Records: Volume VII – The Memoirs of Pre-Han China*. Bloomington: Indiana University Press, 1994.

Nivison, D. 'The Classical Philosophical Writings', in Michael Loewe and Edward Shaughnessy (eds) *The Cambridge History of Ancient China*. Cambridge: Cambridge University Press, 1999. pp.745–812.

Nylan, M. and Thomas Wilson. *Lives of Confucius: Civilization's Greatest Sage Through the Ages*. New York: Doubleday, 2010.

Pines, Y. *The Book of Lord Shang: Apologetics of State Power in Early China*. New York: Columbia University Press, 2017.

Queen, S. and John S. Major (eds). *Luxuriant Gems of the Spring and Autumn*. New York: Columbia University Press, 2016.

Rainey, L. *Confucius and Confucianism: The Essentials*. Chichester: Wiley-Blackwell, 2010.

Sahlins, M. *Confucius Institutes: Academic Malware*. Chicago: Prickly Paradigm Press, 2015.

Shaughnessy, E. *I Ching: The Classic of Changes*. New York: Ballantine, 1996.

Short, P. *Mao: A Life*. London: Hodder & Stoughton, 1999.

Thomsen, R. *Ambition and Confucianism: A Biography of Wang Mang*. Aarhus: Aarhus University Press, 1988.

Turnbull, C. *A History of Modern Singapore 1819–2005*. Singapore: National University of Singapore, 2009.

van Gulik, R. *Sexual Life in Ancient China*. Leiden: E.J. Brill, 1974.

Vogel, E. *Deng Xiaoping and the Transformation of China*. Cambridge, MA: Harvard University Press, 2011.

Watson, B. *Han Feizi: Basic Writings*. New York: Columbia University Press, 2003.

White, H. *The Content of the Form: Narrative Discourse and Historical Representation*. Baltimore: The Johns Hopkins University Press, 1987.

Wong, Y. *Beyond Confucian China: The Rival Discourses of Kang Youwei and Zhang Binglin*. Abingdon: Routledge, 2010.

Xin, G. *Lunyu: Analects of Confucius*. Beijing: Sinolingua, 1994.

Yang, H. and Gladys Yang, eds. *Records of the Historian, Written by Szuma Chien*. Beijing: Commercial Press, 1974.

Yao, X. *An Introduction to Confucianism*. Cambridge: Cambridge University Press, 2000.

Yu, D. *Confucius from the Heart: Ancient Wisdom for Today's World*. [trans. Esther Tyldesley] London: Pan Books, 2010.

Zhao, D. *The Confucian-Legalist State: A New Theory of Chinese History*. Oxford: Oxford University Press, 2015.

NOTES

Abbreviations used: ANA: *Analects*, GL: *Great Learning*, DM: *Doctrine of the Mean*, SDA: *Several Disciples Asked*, KFMA: *Kong Family Masters' Anthology*, LBW: *Annals of Lü Buwei*, MZ: *The Book of Master Mo*, SAMY: *The Spring and Autumn Annals of Master Yan*.

PREFACE TO THE SECOND EDITION (2017)

1 For a demonstration of this thesis at work, see Miller, *The Gongyang Commentary on the Spring and Autumn Annals*, a Han dynasty guide to the original that breaks it down word by word.

2 Hunter, *Confucius Beyond the Analects*, p.13.For a complete list of all extant ancient sources of Confucius, from *The Analects* to mere mentions on fragments of bamboo, see Hunter, pp.39–45.

3 My translations from *The Analects* (Lun Yu), *Great Learning* (Da Xue) and *Doctrine of the Mean* (Zhong Yung) use the Chinese text in Legge, *Confucius*. I similarly give Legge's chapter and verse numbers for my translations of quotes from Mencius.

4 Milburn, *The Spring and Autumn Annals of Master Yan*, p.13.

5 Quotes from both the *Essentials* (Yao) and *Several Disciples Asked* (Er San Zi Wen) are taken from the Chinese text in Edward Shaughnessy's *I Ching: The Classic of Changes*. Quotes from *The Spring and Autumn Annals of Master Yan* are taken from Olivia Milburn's 2016 translation. Quotes from Mozi are taken from Ian Johnston's *The Book of Master Mo*. Quotes from Zhuangzi are from Höchsmann and Yang's *Zhuangzi*, a Kindle edition cited by location, not page.

INTRODUCTION

1 ANA VII, 20

2 ANA XII, 2.

3 ANA VI, 17.

4 ANA II, 1.

5 ANA IV, 13.

6 For a more detailed discussion of the perils of working with Classical Chinese, see my comments in Clements, *The Art of War: A New Translation*, pp.10–12.

7 Yao, *Introduction to Confucianism*, pp.28–9.

CHAPTER ONE

1 Barnes, *Rise of Civilization in East Asia*, p.40 notes that all major oriental languages, including Chinese, refer to the past as something ineffably 'higher' than our present day.

2 Zhao, *The Confucian-Legalist State*, p.202. Uniquely, the state of Qin with its militarised government managed an even greater productivity, 50% again on top of the others' improvements.

3 Pines, *The Book of Lord Shang*, p.14.

4 Shang was the name used by the people of that nation, though their conquerors referred to them as the Yin, and that is the name by which they can be found in most Chinese sources. Chinese sources also cling to the term 'emperor' for the rulers of the period, although I have called them kings here. China's first true emperor was the infamous Qin Shi Huangdi, he of the terracotta army, who was not born until 258 BC.

5 Confucius grew up listening to stories of his ancestor's wisdom in avoiding conflict. He praises his pacifist action in ANA XVIII, 1.

6 Brooks and Brooks, *Original Analects*, p.268, presents a convincing argument that Shuliang was younger, and offers many alternative dates and readings, but I have stuck to conventional belief in this account.

7 Chang, *Life of Confucius*, p.59 is more specific, saying that Mang-pi was 'lame in one leg.' Confucius cared for his brother throughout his life, considering it part of his fraternal duty. During the same period, the people of Sparta were leaving disabled children to die on hillsides. ANA XV, 41, records an incident in which Confucius treats a blind musician with courtesy and compassion, whereas his disciples regard the man as nothing more than a bumbling servant. Confucius's seventy-fifth disciple, Zimie, was said to be Mang-pi's son.

8 Legge, *Confucius*, p.58.

9   Legge, *Confucius*, p.59n. The term *ye-he* as found in the *Records of the Historian* has been variously interpreted as 'torrid,' 'common-law' or even simply as referring to a mating that took place 'in the wilderness.' It is far more likely to refer to their disparity in ages – Zheng-zai was barely fifteen at the time of the wedding, which was young even by the standards of the day. See also Chang, *Life of Confucius*, p.60. Confucius himself regarded the proper age for a girl's marriage as twenty. See Ariel, *K'ung-Ts'ung-Tzu*, p.76.

10 The term *Zhong* optimistically implies 'Second (of Three),' although Confucius proved to be his father's youngest child.

11 Zheng-zai appears to have kept the location of her late husband's grave secret from Confucius, such that at the time of her own death he was unable to bury them side by side for some time. See Yang and Yang, *Records of the Historian*, p.1.

12 ANA XVII, 9.

13 ANA XIII, 5.

14 Chinese sources make the highly unlikely claim of nine feet six inches. Even allowing for the difference in size between an ancient Chinese 'foot' and its modern equivalent, this would still make him seven feet tall! Two metres is thus a conservative estimate, but not unknown in the area. The region of Confucius's birth is now the home of one of China's premier basketball teams.

15 ANA XVII, 25.

16 Duke Zhou, listed throughout this book by his posthumous title of *Zhao*, 'Shining'.

17 Carp is *Li* in Chinese. *Bo-yu* places the character for 'eldest of brothers' ahead of that for 'fish.' See Legge, *Confucius*, p.60.

18 Confucius may have had more children, but these are the only ones recorded. Of the daughters, we know of one because she married a disciple, and of the other because of the inscription on her grave.

19 The clans were descended from the first, second and third sons of a concubine of Duke Huan (r.711–694 BC), and were known in Chinese as the *Shu*, *Zhong* (*Chung*), and *Ji* (*Chi*) families – archaic terms for their ancestors' order of birth. The *Zhong* family later changed its name to *Meng* (Mang) for complex reasons of protocol. At the time of Confucius, it was the Jisun clan that had the greatest influence over affairs of state. See Legge, *Confucius*, p.147n.

20 For example, see ANA III, 1, 6; ANA VI, 7.

21 Mencius, quoted in Legge, *Confucius*, p.60.
22 Ibid.
23 Legge, *Confucius*, p.115. Zilu (Tsze-lû) was also known as Zhong-yu or Ji-lu.
24 Sims, *Confucius*, p.12 claims that Confucius was orphaned at a much earlier age, and that the woman whose death he mourned at this point was an aunt. Nylan and Wilson, *Lives of Confucius*, p.93, cite legends of later centuries that suggested Confucius's odd behaviour regarding his 'mother's' burial suggested that he did not really acknowledge her as his true parent, because he already knew he was the Great Sage.
25 ANA III, 26.
26 *Liji*, II, Section 1.i.10; Section 2.iii.30. Müller/Legge, *Sacred Books of China*, Vol.III, p.369. See also Legge, *Confucius*, p.62.
27 Legge, *Confucius*, p.62. The report of the visit, by the ruler of the small state of Tan, can be found in the *Spring and Autumn Annals*. See Miller, *The Gongyang Commentary*, p.230.
28 ANA III, 23.

CHAPTER TWO

1 Legge, *Confucius*, p.63, places this event in 518. Yang and Yang, *Records of the Historian*, p.2, claim it was when Confucius was a teenager, but they are forced to rely on the scatty ordering of their original Chinese source.
2 Ibid., p.64, discusses who may have accompanied Confucius on his mission.
3 Zhao, *The Confucian-Legalist State*, p.97 observes that reverence for rituals was something of a national stereotype for people from Lu. Confucius fitted right in.
4 ANA XVII, 11.
5 Legge, *Confucius*, p.66, quoting the *Jiayu* or *Narratives of the School*.
6 Ibid.
7 Ibid.
8 Ibid.
9 ANA XI, 12.
10 SDA, 6. Another version of Confucius's encounter with Li Er, the future Laozi, can be found in Höchsmann and Yang, *Zhuangzi*, l.4193 passim, in which Li Er admonishes him: 'Ah, your words are reckless!'

11 LBW, XXVI, 2.2.

12 LBW XVI, 6.5.

13 Barnes, *Rise of Civilization in East Asia*, p.146, notes that horseback riding was not all that common at this time.

14 Legge, *Confucius*, p.67.

15 There was a wall that marked a border between the countries, but on various occasions the border was either too far behind Qi territory, or too deep inside it.

16 Clements, *A Brief History of the Martial Arts*, pp. 24–5.

17 ANA VII, 13.

18 Yang and Yang, *Records of the Historian*, p.3.

19 Legge, *Confucius*, p.68 reports several incidents in the *Jiayu*, but doubts their reliability.

20 Ibid., also quoting from the *Jiayu*.

21 SAMY II, 5.16.

22 SAMY II, 2.5.

23 SAMY II, 2.21.

24 KFMA II, 14. See also Ariel, *K'ung-Ts'ung-Tzu*, p.85.

25 ANA XII, 11.

26 SAMY II, 8.1. A very similar passage, once again putting such words of criticism into the mouth of Yan Ying, can be found in Mozi's chapter 'Against the Confucians', MZ 39.10, and indeed in Yan Ying's biography in *The Grand Scribe's Records*.

27 Legge, *Confucius*, p.69. Legge would rather believe that Yan Ying did *not* say such words, but grudgingly concedes that to many of Confucius's contemporaries, they did indeed sound like fair comment.

28 Yang and Yang, *Records of the Historian*, p.4.

29 ANA XVI, 12.

30 ANA XVI, 6.

31 Ariel, *K'ung-Ts'ung-Tzu*, p.77.

CHAPTER THREE

1 LBW XIX 8.2. The dragon analogy makes this passage immediately seem doubtful. I place it here, rather than after his second reinstatement in later life, because *The Annals of Lü Buwei* specifically refers to him 'accepting a salary' from the Jisun, rather than merely advising them.

2 ANA III, 1.

3 ANA III, 2.

4 ANA III, 3.

5 ANA V, 17.

6 ANA V, 19.

7 ANA XVII, 26.

8 ANA II, 21.

9 ANA VIII, 13.

10 ANA VII, 8.

11 ANA VII, 7.

12 ANA V, 1. The pupil's given name was Gong Ye-chang.

13 ANA VI, 10. The pupil's 'scholar name' was Ziyou. I have kept him as Ran Qiu throughout to avoid confusion with another Ziyou among the disciples.

14 ANA V, 6.

15 ANA XVI, 13. Top Fish's other appearances in Confucian sources are limited to an anecdote in which Confucius admonishes him for mourning his mother for too long, and the later deliberations over the arrangements for his funeral.

16 Or so many of his supporters claim. In fact, however, Confucius seemed to spend most of his life oscillating between careers. On several occasions, he made it very clear he would rather be in government. But see Zhao, *The Confucian-Legalist State*, p.171.

17 ANA II, 2.

18 Mencius II.i.4.3–5. Compare to the Lau translation, *Mencius*, pp.36–7.

19 *Book of Songs/Shi Jing*, Odes of Tang, 'Wu Yi'.

20 ANA IV, 18.

21 ANA IX, 30.

22 Yang and Yang, *Records of the Historian*, p.6. Sources are divided as to when Confucius did what, but it makes sense that he worked on the central canon during this period, and then compiled *The Spring and Autumn Annals* and his annotated *Book of Changes* in his second 'retirement' period a decade later. See Yao, an *Introduction to Confucianism*, p.53.

23 ANA XIII, 3.

24 Guo, *History of Chinese Confucianism*, p.29.

25 Legge, *Confucius*, p.161. The Duke's given name was Song (Sung), but I refer to him throughout this book as *Ding* (Ting) the Decisive, which was his posthumous title. Chang, *Life of Confucius*, p.30, calls him Sung the Serene.

26 Sometimes also called Yang Ho.

27 ANA XVII, 20.

28 See Legge, *Confucius*, p.317n, Nylan and Wilson, *Lives of Confucius*, p.10.

29 ANA XVII, 1. Even in classical Chinese, the passive-aggressive nature of Confucius comes across very strongly here, with simple two-character responses to Yang Hu's florid sentences.

30 Chang, *Life of Confucius*, p.29. On the other hand, Legge, *Confucius*, p.74 claims that Zilu did not get a government post until a couple of years later, *after* Confucius's success at the Jiagu Conference.

CHAPTER FOUR

1 Legge, *Confucius*, p.71n, notes that Zhong-du (Chung-tû) later fell into the hands of Qi, implying that it must have been close to the border. He disregards other sources who claim a more central location for Zhong-du.

2 LBW XVI 5.3.

3 *Liji* VII, i, 8. Müller/Legge, *Sacred Books of China*, Vol.III, p.369.

4 *Liji* VII, i, 8. Müller/Legge, *Sacred Books of China*, Vol.III, p.369.

5 *Liji* I, i, 2. Müller/Legge, *Sacred Books of China*, Vol.III, p.71. Table staff in modern times will be pleased to know that a Confucian gentleman will never treat them with discourtesy.

6 *Liji* I, i, 5. Müller/Legge, *Sacred Books of China*, Vol.III, p.92. This phrase is often misattributed to Confucius himself, but he was merely quoting an older authority.

7 *Liji* I, i, 4. Müller/Legge, *Sacred Books of China*, Vol.III, p.82.

8 Legge, *Confucius*, p.73 is not impressed, calling such tales 'indiscriminating eulogies'.

9 ANA XIII, 15.

10 Yan Hui (Yen Hûi) also known by the scholarly name Ziyuan (Tsze-yüan). See Legge, *Confucius*, p.112.

11 ANA XI, 3.

12 ANA II, 9.

13 ANA VII, 10.

14 Legge, *Confucius*, p.73.

15 Zhao, *The Confucian-Legalist State*, pp.125–6.

16 Legge, *Confucius*, p.73. I have altered his nineteenth century translation slightly in the interests of clarity.

17 Zhao, *The Confucian-Legalist State*, p.171 n.11.

18 SAMY II, 8.6.

19 Legge, *Confucius*, p.74. Once again, I have amended Legge's text slightly. The same story can be found in Xunzi, who also claimed that Confucius was not out of his first week in his justice post before he had courted scandal by ordering the execution of a prominent figure, Yang Hu's brother! See Hutton, *Xunzi: The Complete Text*, pp.318–19.

20 GL, 9, i.

21 ANA XIII, 10. The *Analects* places this speech in a chapter where Confucius is journeying to Wei, implying that his 'three years' is not an objective estimate, but a lament for what he might have achieved if he had been in office for twelve more months in Lu.

22 ANA XIII, 11–12.

23 Yang and Yang, *Records of the Historian*, p.8.

24 Chang, *Life of Confucius*, p.31, makes the logical assumption that it is the ultimate failure of this demilitarisation plan that forced Confucius to resign and leave the country, rather than the nebulous dancing-girl problem offered in most authorities. He offers no historical proof, but since almost every other story of Confucius's life is historical conjecture, I see no harm in repeating his idea here.

25 Legge, *Confucius*, p.65.

26 Yang and Yang, *Records of the Historian*, p.9. Presumably such areas were south of the Qi wall, and hence obviously on territory that was rightfully Lu's.

27 Chin, *Confucius: A Life of Thought and Politics*, p.27, credits Sima Qian with seeing the historical irony – that Qi stepped up its espionage efforts *because* of Confucius's political success.

28 ANA XVIII, 6.

29 Yang and Yang, *Records of the Historian*, p.9.

30 Ibid. For dates to match across different sources, it would appear that it may have taken months for the rot to set in. Brooks and Brooks, *Original Analects*, however, assert that his removal from Lu was simply part of a diplomatic mission to another country, and that he never actually 'resigned'.

CHAPTER FIVE

1 Nylan and Wilson, *Lives of Confucius*, p.3.

2 Legge, *Mencius*, p.365, though the editor thinks this assumption is 'probably incorrect'.

3 ANA XIII, 9.

4 ANA XIV, 20. Ling, the 'Spirit Duke' was the posthumous title conferred upon Yuan, Duke of Wei. See Legge, *Confucius*, p.283n.

5 ANA III, 24.

6 Yang and Yang, *Records of the Historian*, p.10.

7 Nylan and Wilson, *Lives of Confucius*, p.18.

8 Ibid. The same story turns up in Höchsmann and Yang, *Zhuangzi*, 1.4804. The conspiracy theorist in me cannot resist pointing out that Confucius was 'mistaken' for Yang Hu, an officer who enjoyed a meteoric rise during a period in which Confucius was supposedly in seclusion. Could it be that the story of Yang Hu was a later concoction designed to whitewash a period in which Confucius served in office but failed?

9 Ibid.

10 van Gulik, *Sexual Life in Ancient China*, p.31. If Confucius truly were the author of *The Spring and Autumn Annals*, he took great care to note several cases of sexual scandal, and the untimely ends that came to ministers who tried to protest, see also pp.30–32.

11 ANA VI, 26.

12 ANA XVII, 7. The warlord was Bixi (Pi Xi), who had seized control of the town of Zhong-mao (Chung-mau).

13 ANA XI, 25. It is a rare moment in *The Analects*, when Confucius suddenly starts to sound less like a Confucian and more like a Daoist.

14 Named Jiang, ruler of Lu (r.494–468 BC), referred to throughout this book by a translation of his posthumous title *Ai*, or 'Sorrowful'. In the *Liji*, Book XXIV, (p.261n), Legge calls him 'the Courteous, Benevolent and Short-Lived.' The unlucky ruler was predeceased by one of his sons and his favourite wife, according to *Liji* Book II (pp.188–9).

15 ANA VIII, 9.

16 Yang and Yang, *Records of the Historian*, p.15.

17 Ibid.

18 Ibid., p.16.

19 ANA VII, 18.

20 Höchsmann and Yang, *Zhuangzi*, 1.3179. An awful lot of Zhuangzi's anecdotes about Confucius seem to occur in and around the time of his trip to Chu, the country bordering Zhuangzi's native land of Song. An even greater number of anecdotes in *Zhuangzi* centre on his alleged meetings

with Laozi in the capital, which *The Analects* dismisses as little more than a single meeting, while *Zhuangzi* talks it up into what seems to be weeks of intense discussions.

21 Höchsmann and Yang, *Zhuangzi*, l.3083. I have altered the translation of the third line quoted to reflect what, to me, seems like a better fit. I quote from Zhuangzi here, but the same story, more or less can also be found in ANA XVIII, 5.

22 Höchsmann and Yang, *Zhuangzi*, l.4360. But compare to the version of the same incident in Nylan and Wilson, *Lives of Confucius*, p.19, where they suggest it was an assassination attempt by Song agents, determined to make sure that Confucius did not benefit the state of Cao, which he was technically still within the borders of.

23 Yang and Yang, *Records of the Historian*, p.11.

24 Ibid., p.12.

25 ANA V, 25.

26 ANA XV, 1.

27 Yang and Yang, *Records of the Historian*, p.15. After this discussion, Confucius reportedly went to Chen again, but he was back by the summer.

28 Here named for his posthumous title, *Chu*.

29 ANA IX, 12. The repetition is thus in the original classical Chinese, denoting a moment of high emotion.

30 ANA IX, 13.

31 ANA XIII, 24.

32 Yang and Yang, *Records of the Historian*, p.21.

33 Ibid.

CHAPTER SIX

1 All these examples are taken from the relevant years in Miller, *The Gongyang Commentary on The Spring and Autumn Annals: A Full Translation*. For more on the use to the historian of such 'implied editorialisations', see White, *The Content of the Form*, pp.6–7.

2 ANA IX, 2. *The Analects* does not specify a time at which this humorous exchange took place, although Yang and Yang, *Records of the Historian*, p.24, place it in his twilight years.

3 ANA XI, 18. The strange comment is a reference to the custom of sounding a drum in order to call passers-by to listen to a recitation of a criminal's misdeeds.

4 ANA XI, 23.

5 ANA XI, 24.

6 Legge, *Confucius*, p.84.

7 *ESS, 11–12*.

8 ANA XIV, 46.

9 *Book of Rites*, Qu Li I: 12–13.

10 Legge, *Confucius*, p.85; Yang and Yang, *Records of the Historian*, p.24; Chen and Hu, *Zuo's Commentary*, p.1543.

11 Miller, *The Gongyang Commentary on The Spring and Autumn Annals*, p.275.

12 ANA X, 13.

13 *Liji* II.i.3, xxi. (pp.196–7).

14 Chen and Hu, *Zuo's Commentary*, p.1557–61, order events slightly differently.

15 Ibid., p.1558.

16 ANA XI, 8–10.

17 ANA VI, 9.

18 Yang and Yang, *Records of the Historian*, p.25; Legge, *Confucius*, p.87.

19 Legge, *Confucius*, p,87.

20 Chen and Hu, *Zuo's Commentary*, p.1560.

CHAPTER SEVEN

1 Nylan and Wilson, *Lives of Confucius*, p.27.

2 Guo, *History of Chinese Confucianism*, pp.79–84.

3 Lau, *Mencius*, p.77.

4 Lau, *Mencius*, p.35.

5 Hutton, *Xunzi: The Complete Text*, p.337.

6 Hutton, *Xunzi: The Complete Text*, p.60.

7 Hutton, *Xunzi: The Complete Text*, p.328.

8 Zhao, *The Confucian-Legalist State*, pp. 112–3 observes that there were several Hegemons during the late Zhou dynasty, both de facto and de jure. The entire practice, of course, was rendered irrelevant after the last and greatest rise to power of a former dukedom, when the state of Qin conquered all rivals and its ruler proclaimed himself not Hegemon, but Emperor.

9 Pines, *The Book of Lord Shang*, p.12.

10 MZ 39.12. Compare to LBW XIV 6.4 and LBW XVII 3.4.

11   MZ 48.5.

12   Höchsmann and Yang, *Zhuangzi*, l.6813.

13   Watson, *Han Feizi: Basic Writings*, pp.103–104.

14   Watson, *Han Feizi: Basic Writings*, p.107.

15   Lewis, *The Early Chinese Empires: Qin and Han*, p.72.

16   LBW XIV 7.1, LBW XVI 5.3.

17   LBW XIV 4.2.

18   Clements, *The First Emperor of China*, pp.131–2.

19   Guo, *History of Chinese Confucianism*, pp.121–2.

20   Queen and Major, *Luxuriant Gems of the Spring and Autumn*, p.644.

21   Kong, *The House of Confucius*, p.8, for example, calls it the time when her ancestor Confucius's philosophy was adopted as 'the orthodox state ideology'.

22   Zhao, *The Confucian-Legalist State*, p.275 and 302. It's not that Buddhism was the religion of the tax evader, merely that its precepts often incentivised the donation of possessions to monasteries with tax-free status. Monks and monasteries took people and wealth out of circulation in the secular world.

23   Nylan and Wilson, *Lives of Confucius*, pp. 68–9.For those who enjoy playing the numbers game, if Confucius were indeed born in 551 BC, and Great Sages arose *exactly* once every five hundred years, then the most obvious candidate for the new Great Sage was Wudi's great-great grandson Liu Ao, who was born in 51 BC and crowned as Emperor Cheng in 33 BC. Of course, there was no guarantee that he was the one, nor that dates could be so exact. I find it telling that Wang Mang, the usurper who would seize the Han throne in 9AD, was himself born in 45 BC. Close enough?

24   Hunter, *Confucius Beyond the Analects*, pp.306–7.

25   See, for example, Loewe, *A Biographical Dictionary of the Qin, Former Han & Xin Periods*, p.281, which calls him 'little different from the first Qin Emperor' but also praises 'his respect for the ways of the kings of old'.

26   Rainey, *Confucius and Confucianism*, p.140.

27   Guo, *History of Chinese Confucianism*, pp.258–77. The debates and accommodations between the contending schools of Neo-Confucianism span several centuries, and I lack the space for them here, particularly because their ultimate destination is a concentration on the 'Four Books' that form the bulk of the material in my first six chapters! The reader requiring a more detailed study of these issues is directed to the work cited, or Yao's *Introduction to Confucianism*.

CHAPTER EIGHT

1 de Bary and Lufrano, *Sources of Chinese Tradition*, Vol 2, p.266.

2 Nylan and Wilson, *Lives of Confucius*, pp.192–3. Such an ideal was most memorably employed by Wellington Koo, the leading Chinese delegate at the Paris Peace Conference in 1919, who would use it to argue for the return of Shandong province to the Chinese because, among other reasons, as the birthplace of Confucius it amounted to China's 'Holy Land'.

3 Liu et al., *The Birth of Chinese Feminism*, p.123.

4 Nylan and Wilson, *Lives of Confucius*, p.24. As for attempts to bootstrap a progressive Confucius out of what he did, or even what he didn't say, see Foust and Tan, *Feminist Encounters with Confucius*.

5 Lu, *The Real Story of Ah-Q and Other Tales of China*, p.21.

6 Lin, *Confucius Saw Nancy*, pp.44–5.

7 Short, *Mao: A life*, p.27.

8 de Bary and Lufrano, *Sources of Chinese Tradition*, Vol 2, p.342.

9 ANA VII, 15.

10 Rainey, *Confucius and Confucianism*, p.181.

11 ANA XIII, 11–12.

12 Clark, *The Chinese Cultural Revolution: A History*, p.47.

13 ANA XIV, 11.

14 Hunter, *Confucius Beyond the Analects*, p.155.

15 Hunter, *Confucius Beyond the Analects*, p.215.

16 Brooks and Brooks, *The Original Analects*, p.201.

17 Hunter, *Confucius Beyond the Analects*, pp. 6–7.

18 ANA IV 14 and 16, in Brooks and Brooks, *The Original Analects*, p.16.

19 Brooks and Brooks, *The Original Analects*, pp.202–3

20 Brooks and Brooks, *The Original Analects*, p.205.

21 Brooks and Brooks, *The Original Analects*, pp.282 and 264.

22 Hunter, *Confucius Beyond the Analects*, p.315.

CHAPTER NINE

1 de Bary and Lufrano, *Sources of Chinese Tradition*, Vol 2, p.551. The precise degree of shared authorship is difficult to determine. T'ang Chün-i of New Asia College in Hong Kong wrote the initial draft, which was adapted by Carsun Chang in consultation with other contributors, including Mou Zongsan and Hsu Fukuan. The English-language version, however, as excerpted in de Bary and Lufrano, is credited solely to Carsun Chang.

2 ANA VII, 27.
3 Rainey, *Confucius and Confucianism*, p.182.
4 Turnbull, *A History of Modern Singapore*, p.333.
5 Nylan and Wilson, *Lives of Confucius*, p.215.
6 Turnbull, *A History of Modern Singapore*, p.335.
7 Nylan and Wilson, *Lives of Confucius*, p.217.
8 ANA XVII, 2.
9 ANA XV, 14.
10 Turnbull, *A History of Modern Singapore*, p.350; Nylan and Wilson, *Lives of Confucius*, p.216.
11 Nylan and Wilson, *Lives of Confucius*, p.220, cite her inability to translate the classical Chinese *xiao-ren* into modern Chinese as 'petty person', although it is correctly translated in the English-language edition of her work.
12 Yu, *Confucius From the Heart*, p.5.
13 Yu, *Confucius From the Heart*, p.187.
14 Barmé, *China Story Yearbook 2012*, p.69 and p.286.
15 'Confucius in Court', *Global Times*, 14 December 2009.
16 'Avatar pulled from 2-D screens by Chinese government', *Los Angeles Times*, 18 January 2010.
17 Sahlins, *Confucius Institutes: Academic Malware*, p.1.
18 'World Should Watch For Confucius', *China Post*, 1 October 2014.
19 ANA XVI, 4.

Made in the USA
Las Vegas, NV
30 January 2022